Choices are for the Living

Choose A Life Worth Repeating

MICHELE DAVENPORT

authorHOUSE®

AuthorHouse™
1663 Liberty Drive
Bloomington, IN 47403
www.authorhouse.com
Phone: 1-800-839-8640

Published by AuthorHouse 1/27/2012

ISBN: 978-1-4685-0861-1 (sc)
ISBN: 978-1-4685-0860-4 (e)

The time it takes you to look for an excuse is all the time the enemy needs to give you one.

Casting my net for Jesus expecting an enormous catch......Michele Davenport

Lord, as the reader's eyes fall upon the pages of my heart, allow their minds to be open to someone else's truth besides their own; allow Your wisdom to shine through in the midst of my thoughts. Lord, guide the reader to not observe the faults of others but to put a spot light upon their own lives, their own actions, and their own conviction. Lord, may this book bring Glory to Your name and Your name alone.

Walk like you know Him,

Act like you love Him,

Speak like you listen to Him,

Listen like your ears are awake,

Forgive like you need it,

Dare to live your life in fear of the Lord.

Dedication

To Marty, my husband and best friend, I love you. Thank you for becoming the man God created you to be and for encouraging me to become the women God created me to be.

Contents

Acknowledgements

Marty and my girls - for always encouraging me to keep moving forward and pressing in on the things of God. Thank you for the sacrifice of time and the grace to write. I love my family.

To my Goddaughter Alex O'Day- thank you for contributing the photograph you took while on your journey in Scotland. It has made a beautiful front and and back cover.

Jenny Stumpff - for the countless hours you spent editing my book; you were an answer to my direct prayer. Thank you for living with your eyes wide open and your ears fully awake. You are truly an exceptional women of God.

Lori Jonas-thank you for your honesty, your attention to details, and for agreeing to be the third set of eyes on *Choices are for the Living*.

A special thank you to - Kaye Farinella, Allison Muegge, Debi, Lori Jonas and Pastor David Frech for their inspiring testimonies. Revelation12:11, "They overcame him by the blood of the Lamb and by the word of their testimony; they did not love their lives so much as to shrink from death."

Also, I would like to take a moment and acknowledge the lives that have touched my life so deeply by allowing the hand of the Father to paint our stories as one. It has been my greatest honor to be stretched spiritually by the words of their testimonies and the power of their journey. May the many colors of their lives enhance yours in an authentic way.

A Study Guide has been provided at the end of each chapter. It is designed to be done alone or in a small group setting. Also, there is a Weekly Challenge based on the subject of the chapter, along with an Additional Notes: section.

Introduction

C hoices are for the living and the choices we make are made many times out of our emotions, opinions, and life experiences, not necessarily out of the fear of the Lord. What does it mean to fear God? What does that even look like to you? Could it mean to tremble every time you sin? Could it mean shaking when His name is spoken aloud? Or could it possibly mean reading His Word and then doing His Word, according to His Word. Examine the Scriptures for yourself and let them reveal His truth. The word "fear" is written in the NKJV Bible 367 times, and of those 367 times, 118 times are associated in direct fear of the Lord. I wrote this book, not because I have arrived in any way, shape or form at understanding the fear of the Lord, but because I believe it has been misunderstood and therefore ignored. If I could, I would take out the 51 times in the NKJV Scriptures that said, "Do not fear." It would make my goal a lot easier if the Bible did not appear to contradict itself. "Do not fear," then "fear" sounds a bit contrary to the Word. We must distinguish between the two fears, "Do not fear" means "do not fear for I am with you" as it is written in Isaiah 41:10 (NIV). Hebrews 11:7 (NIV) says, "By faith Noah, being warned by God concerning events as yet unseen, in reverent fear constructed an ark for the saving of his household. By this he condemned the world and became an heir of the righteousness that comes by faith." The fear of the Lord actually saved mankind; the whole human race was saved because Noah took God at His Word. God said build an ark and Noah grabbed the nails and went to the wood pile. So, as I journey through the Scriptures to discover the Word of the Lord and how my own fear of Him establishes who I am, I invite you on my journey to discover for yourself the importance of acknowledging the Scriptures.

As your reading my book I will be referencing NKJV, NIV, ESV, and the Message Bible and will provide a list in the appendix of all resources.

Chapter 1

I Don't Want To Be On The Left Side...

Proverbs 1:7, "The fear of the Lord is the beginning of knowledge; fools despise wisdom and instruction."

𝓕 earing the Lord is not something we're into as humans and believers of the Gospel. As a matter of fact, many believers don't understand the fear of the Lord at all. On one hand, many think the fear of the Lord is quivering every time we make a mistake. The reason I decided to write a book on the subject is not that I understand the fear of the Lord to my full capability, or even to yours, but I believe as I am faithful to write, the Holy Spirit will be faithful to teach. I have been a Christian for over twenty years and I have never heard anyone say these words, "I woke up today in great fear of the Lord." We love to infatuate ourselves with His promises, His grace, and His mercy, but when it comes to fearing Him, we quickly quote the 51 times the Scriptures say, "Do not fear," and then ignore the 118 times the Scriptures demand us to be in utter awe and fear of the Lord. We can't get out our kindergarten box of crayons and color God in the image our minds can relate to, nor can we adopt the God of our parents, or even who our church says God is. We need to pick up the Word and read it for ourselves to see who we believe God is. Who is God to you? Stop and think about it for a moment.

We have become nothing more than people pleasers instead of God pleasers. We fear people, situations and statistics more than God. Here are some interesting facts. The Sunday supplement magazine, "USA Weekend," ran a cover story entitled "Fear: What Americans Are Afraid of Today."[1] In a scientific poll, the magazine uncovered the things Americans fear most:

54% are "afraid" or "very afraid" of being in a car crash.

53% are "afraid" or "very afraid" of having cancer.

50% are "afraid" or "very afraid" of inadequate Social Security.

49% are "afraid" or "very afraid" of not having enough money for retirement.

36% are "afraid" or "very afraid" of food poisoning from meat.

35% are "afraid" or "very afraid' of getting Alzheimer's.

34% are "afraid" or "very afraid" of pesticides on food.

33% are "afraid" or "very afraid" of being a victim of an individual violence.

32% are "afraid" or "very afraid" of being unable to pay current debts.

30% are "afraid" or "very afraid" of exposure to foreign viruses.

28% are "afraid" or "very afraid" of getting Aids.

25% are "afraid" or "very afraid" of natural disasters.

After I finished reading this, I quickly realized it appeared Americans did not fear God at all. One of the largest fears in America is being in a car crash. I thought about finding out the statistics on all of the fears and seeing if it was even rational to be fearful of these things, but I decided that was not what this book is about. This book is about fearing God, the Creator of the Universe. It is not about if you should fear those other things, but rather why many of us don't feel it necessary to fear God. Isaiah 66:2 says, "But this is the one to whom I will look: he who is humble and contrite in spirit and trembles at my word." Let me ask you a question, do you tremble at God's Word?

> *How do you respond to Matthew 25:34-46, "Then the King will* **say to those on his right side***, 'Come, you who are blessed by my Father, inherit the kingdom prepared for you from the foundation of the world. For I was hungry and you gave me food, I was thirsty and you gave me drink, I was a stranger and you welcomed me, I was naked and you clothed me, I was sick and you visited me, I was in prison and you came to me.' Then the righteous will answer him, saying, 'Lord when did we see you sick or in prison and visit you?' And the King will answer them, 'Truly, I say to you, as you did it to one of the least of these my brothers, you did it to me.' Then he will* **say to those on the left***, 'Depart from me you who are cursed, into the eternal fire prepared for the devil and his angels. For I was hungry and you gave me no food, I was thirsty and you gave me no drink, I was a stranger and you did not welcome me, naked and you did not clothe me, sick and in prison and you did not visit me.' Then they also will answer, saying, 'Lord, when did we see you hungry or thirsty or a stranger or naked or sick or in*

prison, and did not minister to you?' Then he will answer them, saying, 'Truly, I say to you, as you did not do it to one of the least of these, you did not do it to me.' And these will go away into eternal punishment, but the righteous into eternal life."

Do you look at Matthew 25:34-46 as if these Scriptures apply to everyone else? If you really trembled at His Word, you could not look at these Scriptures and ignore the value of them. You could no longer pass by a man hungry on the side of the road only to get yourself to the other side, or flip the channel when hungry children from Africa come on because it's uncomfortable for you to watch.

After reading and teaching several Bible Studies on "Remembering the Forgotten God," by Francis Chan, I was challenged to live even more accurately according to God's Word. Years before I heard of Francis Chan, I had a heart for the needy in every aspect of the word. I was the lady who held up traffic to give someone a meal. Or if I saw someone on the side of the road in need of prayer, I would stop to pray. I have a tender heart for God's people and I hold myself accountable to His Word. As I taught his Bible study, I grew deeper in the Lord, right along with the ladies taking the class, because "What you have done for the least of these you have done unto me."[2] I had made up my mind to quit playing church like it was an instrument I could pick up and put down at my leisure, and start being the church. To be an instrument that God could use. Have you ever bought a second-hand piano or guitar? Usually when you buy an instrument second-hand, it will need some tuning. Well church, how long will we sit up in the balcony applauding the orchestra and being in awe of the conductor? How long will we just sit in the repair shop, waiting for "church," to be tuned, fixed, restored, pampered and babied before we start living an accurate life according to God's Word?

We are the church, so if we are upset with how things are happening in the church, we should be upset with ourselves. We have all allowed the mimicking, pretending, and the putting on airs; we not only allow it, we are doing it as well. Believers, we are so far off from where the church originated from in the book of Acts. The churches today remind me of the type of house my family and

I used to live in, in Texas. The houses were called "cookie cutter" homes. They only took three months to build, it took longer to go through the paperwork to buy the house than it did to build it. The reason they were called cookie cutter homes was the builder would offer several different floor plans to choose from, but they were all made out of basically the same material, constructed by the same builder, painted by the same painters, bricked by the same brick layers. In other words, the floor plans were a little different, but the houses were more or less the same. This is what I think happened to the local body of Christ. We have made cookie cutter churches. We have used the architect and blueprints of the churches around us, instead of the original architect of the book of Acts.

In Hebrews 11:10 the Scripture says, "For he was looking forward to the city that has foundations, whose designer and builder is God." Sure the churches look a little different on the inside--different music, different programs, different styles of preaching, but basically the same. Nowhere do I find the church of today in the blueprint of Acts. We have strayed from the original plan of God's church for those whose designers and builders are men and not God. I think many pastors have made being a pastor more of a job than a calling. Is the church accurately living Matthew 25:34-46?

Let's reflect again on Matthew 25:40 which says, "And the King will answer them, Truly, I say to you, as you did it to one of the least of these my brothers, you did it to me." Wow!!! You know this means good or bad. Every time we choose to ignore the hurting world around us, we have done this unto Him. Every time we sit around getting fat and happy while investing our money for our future only, instead of investing in a life worth saving, we have done this unto Him. Every time we store our riches up on earth, while ignoring the kingdom of God, we have done this unto Him. Every time we care more about things than people, we have done this unto Him. I am telling you, I understand it like never before. Ever since I taught on "Remembering the Forgotten God" by Francis Chan, the flashlight which I allowed the Holy Spirit to lead me by has turned into a floodlight. I am in this thing with my eyes wide open and my ears fully awake.

Many of us have developed a "no tolerance" policy. We see the hungry man standing on the side of the road, and we turn our nose up as if to say as flippantly as we can, "A man don't work, a man don't eat." Who are you to judge who eats and who doesn't? Do you know the man or women standing on the side of the road? Do you know their situation? Do you know for a fact that they are just being lazy, that they had a job and just up and quit so they could come stand on a street corner and hold up a sign begging for food? My guess would be no, you don't. I would rather stand before my God having fed the hungry than to stand before my God and say something stupid like, "Well I thought they needed to work to eat so I let them go hungry." I decided who ate and who didn't; that was my job. 1 John 4:20-21 says, "For if anyone says, 'I love God,' and hates his brother, he is liar; for he who does not love his brother whom he has seen cannot love God whom he has not seen. And this commandment we have from him: whoever loves God must also love his brother." Your brother is considered to be the one you don't know, maybe someone you have never even seen. "Whatever you did for one of the least of these brothers of mine, you did for me." Have you become a liar? Do you say you love Jesus but ignore the hurting people who surround you every day? If Jesus came back today, what would He find you doing?

Choices are for the Living:

1. Are you on the right side or left side at this moment in your life?

_____
_____
_____
_____
_____
_____
_____
_____
_____
_____
_____
_____

2. What are you most afraid of and why? Do you fear the Lord?

_____
_____
_____
_____
_____
_____
_____
_____
_____
_____
_____
_____

3. What is the first thing you think of when you think of fearing the Lord?

_____

_____

_____

_____

_____

_____

_____

_____

_____

_____

_____

_____

4. Who is the Lord to you?

_____

_____

_____

_____

_____

_____

_____

_____

_____

_____

_____

_____

5. When was the last time you fed a hungry person?

_____
_____
_____
_____
_____
_____
_____
_____
_____
_____
_____
_____
_____
_____

Weekly challenge: Give 5% of your weekly income to your favorite charity, and while there, volunteer.

Additional Notes:

_____
_____
_____
_____
_____
_____
_____
_____
_____
_____
_____
_____
_____
_____

Chapter 2

Yet I Hold This Against You

Revelation 2:4, "Yet I hold this against you..."

*L*et's unpack the Word of God and see what Jesus said to the seven churches, remembering all along, we are the church.

According to the Message translation in the book of Revelation, Jesus is talking to the seven churches, and He says eight times, "Are your ears awake? Listen to the Wind Words, the Spirit Blowing through the churches."[3]

Are we listening, church, are we really listening? Do we have ears that are awake or are we slumbering on the Word of God? Romans 13:11-12 says, "Besides you know the time that the hour has come for you to wake from sleep. For salvation is nearer to us now than when we first believed. The night is far gone; the day is at hand. So let us cast off the works of darkness and put on the armor of light."

Let's see what Jesus said to the seven churches and gleam from the wisdom of the Word.

To the Church in Ephesus, Jesus is saying in Revelation 2:3-6, "I know you are enduring patiently and bearing up for my name's sake, and you have not grown weary. But I have this against you that you have abandoned the love you had at first. Remember therefore from where you have fallen; repent, and do the works you did at first. If not, I will come to you and remove your lamp stand from its place, unless you repent. Yet this you have: you hate the works of the Nicolaitans, which I also hate". Revelation 2:7 (ESV) says, "He who has an ear, let him hear what the Spirit says to the churches. To the one who conquers I will grant to eat of the tree of life, which is in the paradise of God."

To the Church in Smyrna, Revelation 2:10b -11 says, "Be faithful unto death, and I will give you the crown of life. He, who has an ear, let him hear what the Spirit says to the churches. The one who conquers will not be hurt by the second death." The church in Smyrna did not receive a rebuke from Jesus, just encouragement.

To the Church of Pergamum, Revelation 2:14 says, "But I have a few things against you: you have some there who hold the teaching of Balaam, who taught Balak to put a stumbling block before the sons of Israel, so that they might eat food sacrificed to idols and practice sexual immorality." The Pergamum church was compromising the Word of God. Revelation 2:17 says, "He who has an ear, let him hear what the Spirit says to the churches. To the one who conquers I will give some of the hidden manna, and I will give him a white stone, with a new name written on the stone that no one knows except the one who receives it." Historically, a white stone was given to victors at games for entrance to banquets, (cf. the messianic banquet); such a stone was also used by jurors at trials to vote for acquittal.[4]

To the Church of Thyatira, Revelation 2: 19-20 says, "I know your works, your love and faith and service and patient endurance, and that your latter works exceed the first. But I have this against you that you tolerate that women Jezebel, who calls herself a prophetess and is teaching and seducing my servants to practice sexual immorality and to eat food sacrificed to idols." Revelation 2:26-27 says, "The one who conquers and who keeps my works until the end, to him I will give authority over the nations, and he will rule them with a rod of iron, as when earthen pots are broken in pieces, even as I myself have received authority from my Father."

To the Church of Sardis, Revelation 3:1-3 says, "I know your works. You have a reputation of being alive, but you are dead. Wake up, and strengthen what remains and is about to die, for I have not found your works complete in the sight of my God. Remember, then, what you received and heard. Keep it and repent. If you will not wake up, I will come like a thief, and you will not know at what hour I will come against you." Revelation 3:5-6 says, "The one who conquers will be clothed thus in white garments, and I will never blot his name out of the book of life. I will confess his name before my Father and before his angels. He, who has an ear, let him hear what the Spirit says to the churches."

To the Church of Philadelphia, Revelation 3:8 says, "I know your works. Behold, I have set before you an open door, which no one is able to shut. I know that you have little power, and yet you have kept my word and have not denied my name." Revelation 3:12-13 says, "The one who conquers, I will make him a pillar in the temple of my God. Never shall he go out of it, and I will write on him the name of my God, and the name of the city of my God, the New Jerusalem, which comes down from my God out of heaven, and my own new name. He, who has an ear, let him hear what the Spirit says to the churches."

To the Church of Laodicea, Revelation 3:15-17 says, "I know your works: you are neither cold nor hot. I wish you were either one or the other! So that because you are lukewarm, neither hot nor cold, I will spit you out of my mouth. For you say, I am rich, I have

Michele Davenport

prospered, and I need nothing, not realizing that you are wretched, pitiable, poor, blind, and naked." Revelation 3:21-22 says, "The one who conquers, I will grant him to sit with me on my throne, as I also conquered and sat down with my Father on his throne. He who has an ear, let him hear what the Spirit says to the churches."

Let's take a few moments and really examine what Jesus is saying to the seven churches. To the first church Jesus addressed, Ephesus, Jesus said you did well in patience and endurance, but I hold this one thing against you, you have abandoned your first love. Are you still in love with Jesus? Do you remember when you first met Him? Do you remember how excited you were about Him? What has happened to your passion? When I first gave my life to the Lord, I ran around everywhere telling anyone whose ears were awake about my Lord and Savior. My heart would start beating fast, my hands would sweat and I would absolutely feel like I was going to explode with excitement. Have we become complacent with our first love? I have been married for twenty four years and I know complacency can creep in on a marriage, where you just become silent partners. It takes a lot of work to keep the unexpected in your marriage, the astonishing factor happening, the love flourishing daily. Jesus said, "You did well in perseverance and have endured,"[5] but perseverance and endurance does not complete a relationship. I don't want my husband to just endure me; I want him to be crazy out of his mind in love with me. Are you still being astonished by Jesus? Does He still have the Wow factor in your life? What are you having an affair with? What is stealing your time away from your first love? I believe the first step to falling back in love with Jesus is remembering how you felt in the beginning. When we are crazy in love with Jesus, we will be crazy in love with His people. "What you have done to the least of these you have done unto me."

To the church of Smyrna, Jesus was sympathetic. He encouraged them, knowing they were being persecuted. Jesus said "be faithful unto death."[6] What wise words for today as we are living among the dead. Jesus is saying be faithful to Me until your death. Look how many started out in the Spirit but have ended up in the flesh; look how many were on fire for the Glory of the Lord but lost hope and committed adultery on their God. As I look around in the twenty-first century, I see so many faces without a cause, so many faces who wear their name proudly but deny His. I have noticed an increase of self-motivated, self-centered, self-absorbed and self-improvement attitudes. It seems like we took God out of our self and replaced Him with more self. What happened to living for God; when did He become a choice rather than a life style? Oh readers, we read the words to the church of Smyrna and sigh a sigh of relief, but what Jesus was encouraging them to do was to stay faithful unto death. Many of us cannot stay faithful until Monday after Sunday service. No, Jesus did not rebuke them, but He did challenge their thought process--the way they handle persecution. He challenged their natural instincts to deny the Spirit and pick up their flesh and run.

To the church of Pergamum –

> "It was not a commercial city, but its hill formed a natural fortress. It was the seat of the worship of Aesculapius, the god of healing, who was symboled as a serpent, and represented by a live serpent which was kept in his temple. There is a legend about this god to the following effect: On one occasion, in the house of Glaucus, whom he was to cure, while he was standing absorbed in thought, a serpent entered, and twined round his staff. He killed it, and then another serpent came in, carrying in his mouth an herb with which it recalled to life the serpent that had been killed. Aesculapius henceforth used that herb, with healing effects, on man. But an elaborate system of magic grew up around this god, attended with deceptive practices. Pergamum became a focus of idolatrous worship, and could be described as the place "where Satan's seat is." Outward circumstances of temptation, rather than of trouble, are represented in the picture of this church. Under pressure of these temptations the church has partly yielded; but it does not seem to have recognized the seriousness and peril of this partial yielding; and therefore the Living Christ must come to it with the dividing and revealing two-edged sword."[7]

The few things Jesus had against the Pergamum church were some of them were still holding onto the teachings of Balaam, eating food sacrificed to idols, unrestrained feasting or self-indulgence in food and sexual immorality. Many of you reading this book have partly yielded to the Word of God. You think it's tit for tat. I'll do this and God will do that. You are divided between the world and the spiritual. In 1Kings 18:21, Elijah was speaking to the nation of Israel. He was tired of the partial yielding of God's people. Elijah asked them, "How long will you go limping between two different opinions?" How long will we lean into self-indulgence, whether it is with food or sexual encounters? I think there is something definitely wrong when being a virgin until marriage turns men away. Why do we believe if we are living with someone, God is going to bless the relationship? Why do we pray silly prayers of protection when we insist on living our lives partially yielded to God? Many of you drink and drive and then ask God to protect you as if there are no consequences for your sin. Partially yielding to God is limping between two opinions. I do not want to limp on the Word of God. I want to stand boldly and decisively on the Word of God.

Now to the church of Thyatira, although small, it was singled out for this letter of rebuke. This is what Jesus held against the church of Thyatira--they tolerated a woman who called herself a prophetess and was seducing the servants to practice sexual immorality and to eat food sacrificed to idols. Due to a lack of discernment, many fell to her false teachings. I found it interesting that right in the middle of their rebuke, Jesus addressed the ones who didn't hold onto the teachings of Satan. Jesus said, "You did not learn what some call the deep things of Satan."[8] Jesus said, "I do not lay on you any other burden; only hold fast what you have until I come."[9] In other words, bravo, for those who did not learn the deep secrets of Satan, but held fast to the Word of God. A church that stands still is actually moving backwards.

Pastors who tolerate things in their churches so they do not disturb their goals, dreams, or their plans are ways of standing still. We must not care about the numbers, the money, or who we may offend by teaching the unadulterated, uncompromised, unfiltered Word of God. Can I say I don't think we fear God anymore? We fear numbers, people, humiliation and failure. When are we going to make a stand and quit accommodating ourselves and people first, then God? When will we listen to the Holy Spirit and obey? If I took a poll and asked every pastor in America how many times he has received a message to bring forth on Sunday morning from the Holy Spirit, and because he was afraid, he did not preach what he heard or he watered it down so much it didn't resemble what he had previously received from the Holy Spirit. I wonder what the answer would be. Would it be more than 50%?

I think many times we are so focused on the growth of the church that we have dismissed the power of the Spirit. Any church can grow as long as they have some talented people, but what is the motive? Why do we want our churches to grow? So we can store more people in a building to say, "Amen," "Hallelujah," and "Praise be to God," then sit down and do nothing? I would rather have a church of sixty who are on fire for the kingdom of God than a church of a thousand who are complacent, who are satisfied with a menu to choose from instead of the endless buffet God has provided. Sitting is a verb, but the action behind it takes very little effort.

Now to the church of Sardis, "I know your works. You have a reputation of being alive, but you are dead. Wake up, and strengthen what remains and is about to die, for I have not found your work complete in the sight of my God." How many churches (I mean you and me, we make up the church) are appearing to be alive, but we are really dead? Sure, we walk into church on Sunday morning sporting our Sunday best, appearing to be set on fire for Jesus and His work, but the minute we leave the building and there are no more witnesses, we strip off our costumes, put on our worldly clothes and become a dead man walking. Oh yes, my friend, we have a reputation of being alive. We have prayers that are alive. We have all the right words in order and they appear to be alive. We have our Bibles out and our next plan of action on the forefront of our thoughts. We know we will volunteer for the outreach program, and we will teach a class. But are we alive? Are we living a life worth repeating? Are we excited about being a born again, sold out, radical believer for God? Have we as a church been sleeping in the pews only to be awakened by our neighbor who says hallelujah too loud and preaches the pastor's message right along with him. Are you annoyed by how alive the person is who insists on sitting by you? Wake up! Strengthen what remains and is about to die.

Watch out, your sleep is about to lead you to death. Have you ever wondered what happened to the person you saw every Sunday morning in flames for God? One day they were serving God with all their hearts, and the next day they were no more? They fell asleep. It was like a gradual sleep similar to when I choose to read myself to sleep at night. I first get my book, then my glasses, a drink, prop my pillows up, and finally I climb into bed, open my book and begin to read. It is a process, and it takes time. This is what happens to these people, it sneaks in gradually. They started out alive but they are on their way to their spiritual death. One of the dangers of falling asleep spiritually is we leave our watch post unattended, and the enemy can just come in and attack us before we even know what has happened. How many people have fallen asleep in our churches? If you are waiting for your pastor to stir you up, shake you awake or throw ice water in your face, forget it. It is not part of their job. Paul told Timothy, "Stir up the gift in you." [10] In other words, wake up the gift that is in you, Timothy. Wake up from your slumber and quit spending all your effort and strength pretending to be alive when you're really dying. Wake Up!!!

To the church of Philadelphia and to all the other churches, God said, "I know your works," but to the church of Philadelphia, God also said, "I have placed before you a door that no one can shut." [11]God knew their works, so therefore, He said, "I have placed an open door that no one can shut." Wow! What an exciting time for the church of Philadelphia; God had opened a door that nobody could shut. Many people are looking for an open door from God. I myself pray, "Lord open the doors you want me to go through and shut the doors you don't want me to go through." Then we must wait for His time. Let's not just skim by this promise God set before the Philadelphian believers. Let's examine why God would open a door that no one could shut. First of all, God said in Revelation 3:8, "I know that you have but little power, and yet you have kept my word and have not denied my name." God went on to say, "I will make those of the synagogue of Satan who say they are Jews and are not, I will make them come and bow down before your feet and they will learn that I love you. Because you have kept my word about patient endurance, I will keep you from the hour of trial that is coming on the whole world, to try those who dwell on the earth."

Keeping God's Word in the midst of the twenty-first century is challenging to say the least. Not denying His name seems easy, but many of us do it every day without knowing it. If I was a betting lady, I would bet most of us deny His name at least once a day without being aware of how we have denounced the name of Jesus. Every time we pick up a bottle of aspirin for a headache without praying first, we deny the power of His name. You might be thinking, "How can you say that?" Well, every name must bow to the name of Jesus, even the headache must bow to Him. We are blood bought Christians who put more faith in a bottle of aspirin than we do on the Word of God. Have I done this myself? Yes, I have. My goal is faith first, but I too have failed and have denied His name and the power it carries. How else can we deny His name? What about denying His authority in our lives? Can we deny Christ by denying His right to direct our lives? Every time Jesus tells us something to do and we get this stirring in our Spirits, and then we choose not to obey, we deny Christ. The church at Philadelphia was commended for keeping God's Word. Did you know there are approximately 800,000 words in the Bible, all inspired by the Holy Spirit? This is no small feat that the church of Philadelphia had accomplished. And although it appears they had little power, they were able to keep the Word of the Lord and not deny Christ.

Finally, to the church of Laodicea, "I know your works: you are neither cold nor hot." To be lukewarm is like being a plate of potatoes neither hot nor cold; it's just not appealing, it does not taste good. This is what Jesus is talking about when He said, "You make me want to throw up, I want to spit you out of my mouth."[12] This church thinks they have it all--they say I am rich, I have prospered, and I need nothing, not even realizing how wretched they are. They are pitiable, poor, blind, and naked. Lukewarm is a great description of 80% of the people in a 100% of the churches. They come in on Sunday morning not too hot for God, nor too cold. They do just enough to maintain their temperature.

It must take a lot of effort to remain lukewarm, a lot of work to not let something get too cold or too hot. Can you imagine living in a world where people were so in love with God's Word that lukewarm was only used to describe a plate sitting at a restaurant's pickup station too long? Can you envision a church that lives and breathes the Word of God without letting compromise cool down the Word? I am not suggesting that everyone look, act and talk alike. I am suggesting being on fire for God in whatever way that looks like to you. No more lukewarm, no more settling on normal. What has happened to our radical side? Have we grown up so much that it has gotten in the way of radical? Funny, what we consider as radical, was just church two thousand years ago. When did we decide to step out of the Bible and into what everyone else calls normal? When did we let the world, or even the church, tame our passion for the Word of God?

Nothing happened in the Bible in a lukewarm state. They were set ablaze with the power and conviction of the unadulterated Word of God. For example, people were being raised from the dead, people were being healed from Leprosy, blind eyes were being opened, lame people were healed, and all were set free as they abandoned their iniquities. Three thousand were added to the kingdom of God in the book of Acts.

Lukewarm people don't get involved with the people who are on fire; they are spectators not participants. As spectators, they feel they have a right to stifle your heat, to throw water on your fire, and to tell you why it can't be done. They don't get involved; they try to get you uninvolved. Lukewarm people are fantastic dream smashers. They don't acknowledge the Holy Spirit, nor do they live by His directing. If you think about it, hot water added to cocoa mix makes hot cocoa, which is a positive. And when we add cold water to something, like fresh squeezed lemon, we can make lemonade, another positive. But what do you add lukewarm water to in order to get a positive? Come on church, let's look different from what the world looks like. It's sad when people cannot tell the difference between a believer and a non-believer. It's really upsetting when your words need to go before your actions; in other words, when you need to tell people you're a believer because they cannot witness it with your behavior. Within the first five minutes of meeting someone, there should be a noticeable difference in the way they talk, act and represent Jesus. Come on church, Jesus is talking to us. We are the church... may we rise up and shine for His Glory.

Choices are for the Living:

1. If God was addressing the church today, the church being you and me, what do you think His warning to you would be? Resist going any further until you have prayed about the church in you.

_____
_____
_____
_____
_____
_____
_____
_____
_____
_____
_____

2. Have you abandoned your first love? Have you found yourself wearing a leg brace limping between two opinions? Maybe you are lacking in discernment and have fallen into false teaching?

_____
_____
_____
_____
_____
_____
_____
_____
_____
_____
_____

3. Take a long hard look at yourself, as I have done, and examine your walk with your God. Have you become lukewarm in your walk?

_____
_____
_____
_____
_____
_____
_____
_____
_____
_____
_____
_____
_____

4. Are you on the Left side or the Right? Have you become lukewarm on your journey, Explain?

_____
_____
_____
_____
_____
_____
_____
_____
_____
_____
_____
_____
_____

5. Are you walking a walk worth repeating? If not, what can you do to change the carbon copy you are leaving behind?

_____

_____

_____

_____

_____

_____

_____

_____

_____

_____

_____

_____

Weekly Challenge: Go to any coffee shop and buy the person behind you a coffee or a tea. Write down everything you love about Jesus.

Additional Notes:

_____

_____

_____

_____

_____

_____

_____

_____

_____

_____

_____

_____

Chapter 3

My Food Is To Do The Will Of Him Who Sent Me

John 4:34, "My food," said Jesus, "is to do the will of him who sent me to finish his work."

*T*s there a spiritual eating disorder in the body of Christ?

I write a weekly column for a local newspaper. Recently, I wrote a series on the spiritual eating disorder in the body of Christ. I have become painfully aware of the lack of faith with action in the body of believers. I have seen complacency in the body of Christ. It's almost like some of us are living while only waiting to die. It's like we don't believe what we say we believe. Have we become desensitized to the Word of God. How can that be? How can we look at His Word and feel nothing? How can we get up in the morning, get ready for our day, eat breakfast, check our e-mails, blackberries, and Facebook, then kiss the family good-bye, but never even glance in God's direction or pick up the written Word? It's as if we have made God an option. The Lord gave me an amazing revelation the other day. He said, "Michele there is a "U" and an "I" in the word UNITY. If the "U" and "I" don't agree, it's like two trying to walk together without agreeing to meet."

How can we walk together with God if we insist on limping between two opinions--ours and His? God says it is better to serve than to be served, but the absence of fearing the Lord is so prevalent in the body, that we have somehow made this a suggestion rather than the Word of God. If we read the Bible and its words are too difficult to digest, then we re-write it in the mind of the listener. For example, the Lord commanded us in John 15 to "love each other as I have loved you." Do we love each other the way God loves us? I think we would be hard-pressed to say we like each other the way God loves us. Some of us have become masters of manipulation; we manipulate the Word of God to fit our own beliefs instead of changing our thoughts to match His. Another example of us re-writing the Word of God is found in Matthew 6. The Word clearly says *when* you give, *when* you pray and *when* you fast, but again we are tempted by the flesh of our own digestive system to assume God meant *if* we give, *if* we pray and *if* we fast. If I am wrong about this, ask yourself one question - when is the last time you gave to the needy, fasted or prayed? Have you made this an option or a general request from a God whom you do not fear? I found it interesting that over 13.9 million self-improvement books were sold in 2008. Imagine what the numbers are now?[13] Why do we insist on seeking what has never been lost? We read books and read books until we find someone who agrees with us.

John 4:34, "my food, said Jesus, is to do the will of him who sent me and to finish his work."

I believe there is a great threat to the twenty-first century church. What is the threat? A spiritual eating disorder running rampant in the body of Christ which has left our churches filled with four types of believers: bulimic believers, anorexic believers, obese believers and the radical believers. First, I would like to take a look at the bulimic believer. A bulimic believer eats and eats the Word of God until they disagree with the Word, or until the Word becomes uncomfortable, or costs them something they're not willing to give. Oh sure, the bulimic believer eats up 1 John 1:9, "If we confess our sins, he is faithful and just and will forgive us our sins and purify us from all unrighteousness." But the bulimic believer will purge out Mark 11:25, which says, "And when you stand praying, if you hold anything against anyone, forgive him, so that your Father in Heaven may forgive you your sins." For the bulimic believer, it's an all you can eat buffet when it comes to John 3:16, "For God so loved the world that He gave His one and only Son, that whoever believes in Him shall not perish but have eternal life." Yes, we say, "Praise be to God" on that one, but we purge out the very words of Jesus in Matthew 22:37-39, "Love the Lord your God with all your heart and with all your soul and with all your mind. This is the first and greatest commandment. And the second commandment is like it; Love your neighbor as yourself." Are you getting the point?

Bulimic believers sit in church week after week, month after month, year after year, and eat, and eat, and eat, but when it's time to act on what they have eaten, they purge the very Word that was sent for their nourishment. For an example, in your physical body you need to eat certain things to give your body the proper amount of nutrition, to nourish and fuel your body so it can run at its optimal best. There are certain foods that I really don't like, but because I know my body needs them, I eat those foods in spite of the fact that I have not acquired a taste for them. The same analogy can be applied to the spiritual body. You may not like every bite of what the Bible has to offer you, but because you know it's good for your spiritual well-being, you partake just the same. In Ezekiel 3:1-3 the Word says, "And he said to me, 'Son of man, eat what is before you, eat this scroll; then go and speak to the house of Israel.' So I opened my mouth, and he gave me the scroll to eat. Then he said to me, 'Son of man, eat this scroll I am giving you and fill your stomach with it.' So I ate it, and it tasted as sweet as honey in my mouth." In Ezekiel's vision, he ate the Word of God and it tasted like honey. In ancient times, books were usually scrolls and one page could be up to thirty feet long. Most of the time, the writings were on just one side, but not in this case; in this case, the writings were on both sides. The warning overflowed to show the measure of the judgment. We must eat both sides of the Word of God not just the side buttered with what is easy to digest.

How many of you really "love your God with all your heart, with all your soul, and with your entire mind" [14] enough to digest even what we would rather purge. I always thought this Scripture said, "With all your might," but no it says, "with your entire mind." How can we love God with our entire mind? By choosing what we allow to occupy our thoughts, by making a conscious choice on what we are meditating on. What does your mind spend most of its time on? I know when I fell in love with my husband, I could not keep my mind off of him. I thought about him day and night. When you're in love, you will do anything to be with that person; you will go out of your way just to spend a moment alone with them. When is the last time you went out of your way to spend time with your first love? When is the last time you woke up early just to sit quietly with your God? This is the first of the greatest commands, and the second is "love your neighbor as you do yourself." Oh, for the bulimic believer, it says in Revelation 2:4-5, "Yet I hold this against you: You have forsaken your first love. Remember the height from which you have fallen! Repent and do the things you did at first." Believers, if you will love your Lord with all your heart, with all your soul, and with your entire mind, loving your neighbor as yourself will follow.

Don't go to church to take up a seat and to fill your stomach with only what is comfortable to swallow. Allow God to fill you with His spiritual food so you too can accomplish the will of God in your life.

Now let's look at the next eating disorder in the body of Christ, the anorexic believer.

> *James 1:23-25, "Anyone who listens to the word but does not do what it says is like a man who looks at his face in a mirror and after looking at himself, goes away and imme-*

diately forgets what he looks like. But the man who looks intently into the perfect law that gives freedom, and continues to do this, not forgetting what he has heard, but doing it, he will be blessed in what he does."

The anorexic believer goes to church every week, sitting in the same place, talking to the same people, and remaining in the same mindset they were in the week before, never really occupying the Word of God. Oh sure, they say a couple of "Amen's," throw in a few "Praise the Lord's," and for show, why not a "Hallelujah" as well. But as they leave the building, get into their cars and put their Bibles in the back seat, they remain untouched by the Word of God. An anorexic believer never really partakes in the actual eating of God's Word. They feed off the desires of their flesh. Oh, they will hardly miss a Sunday, their attendance is almost perfect, but no one is ever changed by their presence. They remain the same, their world remains the same, and their existence is complacent. Will they go to heaven? I am sure they might, but will they take anyone with them? No, probably not.

How can we look in the mirror and forget what we look like? The same way we can listen to a message and remain the same. The anorexic believer is starving to death because the world is feeding them a man-made diet consumed with self. They have become cannibals, in a sense, because they feed off each other instead of the Word of God. Can I be as bold as to say that maybe the anorexic believer has cared more about the appearance of being in the body Christ instead of a true authentic relationship with the body of Christ? Has church become nothing but a social event where you show off your latest dress or gather around the coffee pot and talk about who's going to win the next fantasy football league? Do you think just because you show up, God is pleased? Even the devil shows up at church! Oh, maybe someone is taking attendance, but I don't think it amounts to anything if you become just another check in a box.

The Apostle Paul said in Philippians 3: 7-11, "but whatever was to my profit I now consider loss for the sake of Christ. What is more, I consider everything a loss compared to the surpassing greatness of knowing Christ Jesus my Lord, for whose sake I have lost all things. I consider them rubbish, that I may gain Christ and be found in him, not having a righteousness of my own that comes from the law, but that which is through faith in Christ—the righteousness that comes from God and is by faith. I want to know Christ and the power of his resurrection, the fellowship of sharing in his sufferings, becoming like him in his death, and so, somehow, to attain to the resurrection from the death."

Paul was saying whatever I valued before pales in comparison to Christ. I consider it all rubbish, nothing but a pile of dog dung, chicken poop, a litter box filled with rubbish. I consider it all worthless waste. Everything I have done, everything I have accomplished, any money I have earned, anything I have bought, any education I have accumulated, I consider it all rubbish compared to my relationship with Christ. Can you say I find it all rubbish in comparison to my relationship with Christ? Can I? Whatever you do first thing in the morning holds the most value in your heart. Stop right here and ask yourself what do I really value? What do I spend my time doing? Does God own a place in your life in addition to Sunday mornings?

There are 168 hours in a week; who and what gets the other 166 hours left in the week when you're not at church? What have you replaced God with? Has it furthered eternal fulfillment to anyone else's life? If Jesus came back today, would He be pleased with what you are accomplishing for His kingdom? Are you an anorexic believer? Matthew 13:44 says, "The kingdom of heaven is like treasure hidden in a field. When a man found it, he hid it again, and then in his joy went and sold all he had and bought that field." Wow! Did the Word of God say in his joy, he sold everything he had to purchase the field? Most of us are not willing to give up a date night to bless someone else, much less sell everything if God asked us to. The amazing thing is--He is worth it. Isaiah 6:1-4 says, "In the year that King Uzziah died, I saw the Lord seated on a throne, high and exalted, and the train of his robe filled the temple. Above him were seraphs, each with six wings: With two wings they covered their faces, with two they covered their feet, and with two they were flying. And they were calling to one another: 'Holy, holy, holy, is the Lord Almighty; the whole earth is full of His glory.' At the sound of their voices the doorposts and thresholds shook and the temple was filled with smoke."

Readers, is this the God you serve? Is this the God you see when you're praying, believing and bombarding heaven for your petitions of unanswered prayers? Have you made God less than what He is? "His robe filled the temple, the angels are in constant praise of His name, calling out to one another, holy, holy, holy, is His name as the temple shook and was filled with smoke."[15] This is the God we serve, not some wimp who sits on a teeter-totter, rocking back and forth, content with our walk.

This God is the same God who is confronting the rich man In Mark 10. In Mark 10:17-19, the rich man was asking Jesus what to do to inherit eternal life. Jesus told him, "you know the commandments: do not murder, do not commit adultery; do not steal, do not give false testimony, do not defraud, and honor your father and mother." Mark 10:20-22 says, "'Teacher,' he declared. 'All these I have kept since I was a boy,' Jesus looked at him and loved him, 'One more thing you lack,' he said, 'Go sell everything you have and give to the poor, and you will have treasure in heaven. Then come and follow me.' At this the man's face fell. He went away sad, because he had great wealth."

I noticed several things. The first thing I noticed was Jesus looked at him and loved him. In other words, Jesus was not suggesting he sell everything because He was trying to punish the rich man. No, He knew if the rich man's heart was not right, his walk would not be right either. God cares more about our relationship with Him than our possessions. This is sad because I think most of us care more about our possessions than we do about God. Oh, we will say we don't, but what do we spend most of our time doing? Where your money is there you will find your heart. What do you spend your money on?

The second thing I noticed was the rich man appeared to be awesome at keeping some of the commandments. Jesus only mentioned the last six, but He left out the first four. I began to ponder on this fact. Why? I believe He only mentioned the ones the rich man was keeping. Isn't this how we as modern day twenty-first century Christians think? As long as we are not stealing, murdering, committing adultery, not coveting, giving a false testimony or dishonoring our parents, we are pretty good Christian folk. What about not having any other gods before Me, or do not make for yourself an idol, in addition to do not misuse the name of the Lord your God, and remember the Sabbath day and keep it holy.

I want to address the first commandment today: Do not have any other gods before Me. I believe the rich man's face fell because he had another god before the one true God—money, a false sense of security. It broke his heart to think that all he had worked for, all his stored up treasures and all which defined him, Jesus wanted him to give away. Jesus wanted him to be sold out for the cause. Maybe Jesus wanted him to acknowledge the fact that money had taken him captive and held him prisoner with his own wealth. It had handcuffed him to self-indulgences while others starved to death. Maybe Jesus was saying to the young rich man - it doesn't matter if you gain the whole world, if in the process, you lose Me, it's all for naught.

In Luke 16, Jesus tells of a story about another rich man and a beggar whose name was Lazarus . Lazarus lay at the gate begging, while covered in sores and longing to eat the scraps from the rich man's table. Finally the beggar died and the angels came and carried him away. The rich man died as well and was buried in hell where he was tormented. He looked up and saw Abraham and said, "Have pity on me and send Lazarus to dip his finger in the water to cool my tongue." Abraham replied, "Son, remember in your lifetime you received your good things, while Lazarus received bad things, but now he is comforted here, and you are in agony.[16]"

Wow! Readers, this is a serious consequence for ignoring the poor outside your gate. I can hear many of you thinking, "Thank God I am not the rich man," but the truth is, you are, and so am I. Let me share something shocking with you. At least 80% of humanity lives on less than $10.00 a day and 48% live on $3.14 a day. 25% live on $1.72 a day. [17] Now the question is what are we going to do about it? Who are the poor outside your gate? Do you just walk by with the attitude, "That's not my problem"? Do you think to yourself, "I wish I could help but I'm having a hard enough time taking care of my own family?" Or are you among those who are blinded by the darkness of self? If I give, I might not have enough for my family, or what about my future, who is going to take care of me when I retire? Let me have the honor of answering that question, the same God who is supplying your needs. Now if you're not in the 25% of people making $1.72 a day, you are considered the rich man. The anorexic can't eat the Word of God because they are too busy eating off the desires of their flesh, nothing more than a cannibalistic believer.

The first spiritual eating disorder we discussed was the bulimic believer, who only digests what they want to believe, only what they are comfortable consuming, only what can be explained, and then ultimately, they purge everything else out. Next, we discussed the anorexic believer. This kind of believer never really partakes in the actual eating of God's Word. They feed off the desires of their flesh, cannibalism if you will, which leads them to spiritual starvation. Now, I would like to address the obese believer. The obese believer becomes stationary in their walk with Christ, they become idle.

2 Thessalonians 3:11says, "we hear that some among you are idle. They are not busy; they are busybodies." An obese believer is always eating but never exercising their authority in Christ. They are all consuming with the Word, but are not doers of the Word.

Ezekiel 33:30 -32 says, "As for you, son of man, your countrymen are talking together about you by the walls and at the doors of their houses, saying to each other, 'Come and hear the message that has come from the Lord.' My people come to you, as they usually do, and sit before you to listen to your words, but they do not put them into practice. With their mouths they express devotions, but their hearts are greedy for unjust gain. Indeed, to them you are nothing more than one who sings love songs with a beautiful voice and plays an instrument well, for they hear your words but do not put them to into practice."

An obese believer fills themselves with so many different things--their possessions, entertainment, jobs, social events, homes and cars. When the day has come to an end, the last light has been turned off, they are snuggled down in their beds and left feeling over-stuffed with the world. They are anxious, angry and full of anxiety. An obese believer hears the Word, thinks it has a beautiful sound, tells everyone about the great Word of God but never acts on what they hear.

I would like to share a very personal story. One Tuesday night, I went to teach my class on the Holy Spirit and the ladies and I were led to go to our local hospital to pray for those who had loved ones residing there. After we had finished praying, I felt led to buy some food for the needy. The ladies and I searched for someone who appeared to be homeless and hungry, but by that time of night, I guess they had already found refuge for the evening. I explained to the ladies that I had many homeless and hungry people out in the direction I lived, and I would distribute the food on my way home. We said our good-byes and got into our vehicles to go our separate ways. As I was driving home, I began praying and singing in the Spirit, and then the words, "Lead me, oh Lord, lead me to the needy" came to my mind. Directly after I prayed, I remembered a man passing me by on his motorcycle. I noticed his bandana flying off. I was going to stop and pick the bandana up for him if I saw him brake. I did not see him brake that night. Within a few minutes, I was kneeling beside him, praying for him, as I laid my hand on his back calling on the name of my Jesus. I continued to stay with him and pray until the ambulance arrived, and then I was asked to step away. From a distance, I continued to pray because in Matthew 25:35-46, Jesus said, "everything you have done unto them you have done unto me." I didn't know this man's name at the time, and I didn't know if he was married or if he had children. I didn't know if his parents were still alive or if he had siblings, or grandchildren, but what I did know was this man was God's son and I was not only compelled, but driven, to pray for God's son on that night. As I stood in the moment which seemed to engulf me, a nurse who had been there with me asked me if I would like her to go check on him. I said, "Yes, would you please?" She left for just a moment and then reported back that he had not made it. Oh, how my heart broke for the man on the motorcycle that belonged to God. As I stood in silence while all the noise of uncertainty was developing around me, all I could hear was the Spirit of God saying, "Michele sometimes I will lead you to the hungry, and sometimes I will lead you to pray for strangers in a hospital and sometimes, Michele, I will lead you to a man dying on the road." I knew from that point on, my existence would never be the same. I want to be led by the Spirit for the rest of my life into eternity. The ladies and I have talked since this happened, and we have come to the conclusion that every step we took that night led me to the man I now know as Robert. God cared so much about His son that He made sure Robert was not alone when he made the transition from this life to the next. Thank you for letting me share my one and only memory of the man on the motorcycle named Robert.

Can you ignore God's Word? Yes you can, but who will remain untouched because you did? If this doesn't make you want to listen and obey the Spirit of God who lives in you to direct and lead you into all truth, to be your comforter in your time of need, to give you wisdom, freedom, peace, understanding, boldness, rebirth and a reborn cleansing, then you are left to your own demise.

As the night went on and I had finally made it home embodied in my thoughts, I remembered the questions I had been asking on Tuesday nights. I would begin each class with three questions. The first question I asked the ladies- are they willing to be an answer to someone else's prayer? The second question I asked the ladies - are they willing to follow the Holy Spirit without knowing where He is leading? The third and last thing I would ask was not only a question but a challenge - to treat everyone they see like they were Jesus. Because "what you have done for the least of these you have done unto me." The obese believer hears the Word, thinks it has a beautiful sound, tells everyone about the great Word of God, but never acts on what he hears. He is a hoarder of the Word. Stop right here and ask yourself this question, "Would you have stopped for the man on the motorcycle?" If you had to think about your answer, or think of an excuse for your answer, then maybe you are too stuffed with the food of this world to make a difference in the next. An obese believer who fills his self up with the cares and worries of this life, will be too full to inhale all of what the Holy Spirit has in store for him. Our purpose is to live out loud on purpose for our Christ Jesus.

Many of you may be asking yourself which believer am I? I have asked myself the same question. Well, to be completely honest, I have the potential to be any one of the three believers at any given time if I do not stay connected, plugged in and fastened to the hip of the Holy Spirit. Which believer are you? My goal is to be the radical believer, radically serving God in an untraditional way.

I want to discuss the last believer which is the radical believer. I thought about writing on the balanced believer. It matched, but only in words. I do not want to be a balanced believer. I want to be an untraditional, sold out, radical, on fire, willing to be led by the Holy Spirit even if I do not know where He is leading me, kind of a believer. I want to strike a match in the heart of God's people wherever I go. I want to make a difference in a place where being the same has been accepted as "fitting in," but in reality, if we were to examine the truth, it's only living with a compromised standard.

I do not want to compromise the Word of God any longer. Ironically, what I call a radical believer, the book of Acts calls the church.

> 2 Timothy 3:1-5 says, "But understand this, that in the last days there will come times of difficulty. For people will be lovers of self, lovers of money, proud, arrogant, abusive, disobedient to their parents, ungrateful, unholy, heartless, unappeasable, slanderous, without self- control, brutal, not loving good, treacherous, reckless, swollen with conceit, lovers of pleasure rather than lovers of God, having the appearance of godliness, but denying the power."

The Apostle Paul was in prison in Rome awaiting his death when he wrote this letter to Timothy. He was not talking to unbelievers but believers. Paul was talking about the church. People will attend the church because they love themselves, instead of God. You might be thinking that is a bold statement, but why do people love money? Because they love themselves. Why are people abusive? They love themselves; they want their way and if they don't get their way they become abusive. Why won't people forgive others? Because it is about themselves not others. Listen, I know there is real relevant pain out in the world. I know people have been sexually, mentally, verbally and physically abused, so how could I say that it is selfish not to forgive? Because I myself have been sexually, mentally, verbally and physically abused, and until I released those people, I always had my mind on myself. Some people say, "I just cannot control myself." The only reason they cannot control themselves is because they want what they want no matter what it costs to get it. Every word the Apostle Paul wrote in 2 Timothy 3:1-5 is about people being lovers of self, but the book of Acts is the exact opposite. How can we strike a match and light up a room if we are making it all about self? How can people see the Holy Spirit in you if it's all about self? How can we call ourselves followers if we will not follow? Let's step into the book of Acts for a moment and nail our tent pegs to the ground and see what the Lord shows us.

> Acts 2: 42-47 (ESV), "And they devoted themselves to the apostles' teaching and the fellowship, to the breaking of bread and the prayers. And awe (reverent fear) came upon every soul and many wonders and signs were being done through the apostles. And all who believed were together

and had all things in common. And they were selling their possessions and belongings and distributing their proceeds to all, as any had need. And day by day, attending the temple together and breaking bread in their homes, they received their food with glad and generous hearts, praising God and having favor with all people. And the Lord added to their number day by day those who were being saved."

If we want our churches to grow, we must be different, we must look different, we must act different, and we must walk and speak different. You cannot change and remain the same. You cannot keep doing the same thing to get a different result. Most churches will undoubtedly say they want the power of God in their churches, but they are not willing to do what it takes to receive the power that the church of Acts had. What did you read when you read the account in the book of Acts? It seems to me they were in complete unity. No one was above and no one was beneath. It seemed to me they did not put one person on a pedestal and another underneath the pedestal. They honored each other. They were not fighting about who was going to be in a spotlight, but rather, they put the spotlight on Jesus. They cared for the people more than they did themselves. It wasn't about who had what gift or the number of people who showed up, but rather, about unity and the breaking of bread in the homes. I am not talking about communism. The people still had personal possessions and houses to live in. I'm talking about the desire to give to one another out of a place of love.

We were in the military for 25 years and we have had many opportunities to visit numerous churches, but one church has a place in the forefront of my thoughts--not because of a person but because of a method. Here is the method they used: you, (the church goers) would go to church Sunday morning and then on Sunday evenings you would obtain the pastor's notes, then meet in different homes with a home group leader in that area to discuss the message that was brought forth that morning. The objective was to talk about how you could use what you had learned on Sunday morning in the upcoming week which would preserve the people from becoming complacent with the Word of God.

If we are going to make a difference we must **be different**, we must walk by the Spirit. Recently, my dad and aunt called and asked if they could meet us for lunch at Longhorn Steakhouse, and we said, "Yes." As we were sitting talking to our waitress, she mentioned that she had some unexpected car repairs. After we had placed our order and our waitress left, my aunt and I decided that we should take up an offering to help our waitress with her repairs. Why am I sharing this with you? I am sharing this because we must live by the written Word of God. We cannot ignore Matthew 25:35-46 any longer, "what you have done to one of the least of these you have done unto me." I want to live the Bible out-loud for Jesus. I want my life to be relevant. To only live and breathe is to die a slow death, but to save the dying while living makes every breath I breathe worth inhaling...

Choices are for the Living:

1. What kind of believer are you? The bulimic, anorexic, obese or the radical?

   _____
   _____
   _____
   _____
   _____
   _____
   _____
   _____
   _____
   _____
   _____
   _____
   _____

2. What are you purging out in order to meet your selfish desires?

   _____
   _____
   _____
   _____
   _____
   _____
   _____
   _____
   _____
   _____
   _____
   _____
   _____

3. When is the last time you gave to the needy, or when was the last time you fasted, or prayed?

_____
_____
_____
_____
_____
_____
_____
_____
_____
_____
_____
_____

4. If you missed several Sunday services in a row, would anyone be affected by your absence and why or why not?

_____
_____
_____
_____
_____
_____
_____
_____
_____
_____
_____
_____

5. Do you spend more time thinking about what you're going to wear, or what time the game starts on Sunday morning than you do about the people you have the potential to minister to?

_____

_____

_____

_____

_____

_____

_____

_____

_____

_____

_____

_____

_____

Weekly Challenge: Fast for one day and seek God about how you can be an answer to someone else's prayer. For example, maybe a neighbor is going out of town and you could offer to check their mail or mow their grass while they're gone. Or maybe one of your friends has an anniversary coming up--you could offer to keep their kids overnight. Or maybe a friend lost their job--you could buy them a gift card at the grocery store. Another idea would be to make someone a homemade dinner that has been under the weather or working hard lately.

Additional Notes:

_____
_____
_____
_____
_____
_____
_____
_____
_____
_____
_____
_____
_____

Chapter 4

For This Is The Whole Duty Of Man

Ecclesiastes 12:13-14, "Now all has been heard; here is the conclusion of the matter: Fear God and keep his commandments, for this is the whole duty of mankind. For God will bring every deed into judgment, including every hidden thing, whether it is good or evil."

$\mathcal{B}$ e prepared to be a light on a mountain, a city on a hill to shine before the coming of Christ. "'And he will go on before the Lord, in the spirit and power of Elijah, to turn the hearts of the fathers to their children and the disobedient to the wisdom of the righteous - to make ready a people prepared for the Lord.' Zechariah asked the angel, 'How can I be sure of this? I am an old man and my wife is well along in years.' The angel answered, 'I am Gabriel. I stand in the presence of God, and I have been sent to speak to you and to tell you this good news. And now you will be silent and not be able to speak until the day this happens, because you did not believe my words, which will come true at their appointed time'" (Luke 1:17-20).

I pray you get a hold of these truths, readers. Gabriel was sent by God to reveal the birth of John the Baptist. John's purpose was to prepare the way for Jesus. I think it is noteworthy to mention the different responses Gabriel received when he showed up to bring a Word of the Lord forth. In Daniel 9:21, Daniel believed and acted on the Word of the Lord; he began to fast and pray for the people of Israel. When Gabriel approached Mary, the future mother of the Messiah, she said these simple but profound words, "May it be to me as you have said." [18] Oh, how the Lord desires our faith to hold hands with our obedience.

In Luke 1:11-20, Zechariah said, "How can I be sure of this?" He was silenced because of his unbelief. I wonder how many of us have become mute because of our unbelief. How many times does something come up in the Word of God, but because you don't understand it, you reject it? Gabriel said John would be born of a purpose (as we are also). Ephesians 2:10, "For we are God's workmanship, created in Christ Jesus to do good works, which God prepared in advance for us to do." His purpose was to turn the hearts of the fathers back to their children, and the disobedient to the wisdom of the righteous, to make ready a people prepared for the Lord. Let me ask you a question, readers, where are you on this spectrum? Are you the fathers that need to turn their hearts back to their children? Or could it be, you are the disobedient? God has given you a Word but all you can say is, "How can I be sure of this?" Maybe it's neither, maybe you just need to surrender so you can help prepare the people for Jesus' return. There is a lot of harvesting to do so please don't become self-satisfied with your own salvation. We must surrender our agendas as to how and when we think things should be done. In addition, we must submit to God's plans for our lives and lay down our narrow thinking.

Many of us think life is about going to work, paying the bills, raising the kids, and what is left over is our free time. Yes, all of these things are a part of our lives, but many of us have forgotten our main job which is to be preparing the way for Jesus' return, to bring as many as we can along with us, to leave no man, woman or child behind. We are to be a light on the hill, but some think we are only to occupy the hill. Remember in Luke 5:4 – 5 (NKJV) when Peter was in the boat. He had been fishing all night to no avail, and God said "lay down your nets," but he laid down "a net," instead of "nets." Peter did not put down all that he had, only some, and his net broke. Peter did not lay down what the Lord said to lay down. Hear me readers, our priorities must be shifted for us to surrender to our Lord. Let's lay down what He says to lay down and pick up what He says to pick up.

Let's not take surrendering lightly; Zechariah was muted because he could not surrender to the Word of the Lord. Let's commit to walking it out on a path worth repeating, leaving manna (Bread) behind so you can lead others. Sit in silence or choose to believe the Word of the Lord. Faith has a mouth. If we really feared God, we would do the greatest command - love others as we love ourselves. Do you? **The whole duty of man is to fear God and keep His Commandments**.

What has God commanded you to do? Listen readers, if you don't know the answer to this question then you can rest assured you're not keeping His commandments. Matthew 22:37-40 says, "Jesus replied: Love the Lord your God with all your heart and with all your soul and with all your mind." This is the first and greatest commandment. And the second is like it: 'Love your neighbor as yourself.' All the Law and the Prophets hang on these two commandments." Do you realize the greatest command is to love? Stop and think about love for a moment. Do you really live like you believe the greatest command is love? It seems like lately more than ever before, I am witnessing people who are walking in irritation, aggravation and segregation. You might be thinking how could I make such a statement about the population in general? Well, I have been watching people, and even though we are not at war with the

Michele Davenport

racial issues at this time, there have definitely been segregations in the body of Christ. Many "Christians" have segregated themselves so far from the world that they can't remember the last time they were a witness of God's goodness outside their normal realm of people.

It saddens me to think that some of the believers have become a "click;" they have become no more than a social organization. We are called to the call of love without our homemade borders, without our separate water fountains or special seating arrangements. Why don't you cross over your town's borders to witness to the other side? Why don't you try going down to the inner city and drink from a fountain the homeless may drink from and sit among what the world calls outcasts? Why not take the subway one day and see what God does? I would like to share with you a few times the Lord has challenged me to obey His command to show love to others in a unique way.

I remember one time as I was driving to church to teach a class, I was praying in the Spirit with interpretation. As I was praying and singing unto the Lord, the words that kept coming out were, "Oh, how I want to be used by You, Lord. Oh, how I want Your will in my life. Show me what to do and I will do it Lord."

I had to take an alternate route because of road construction and the route I had to take was through the "ghetto," an area known for drugs, crime and violence. As I was driving through this neighborhood, I came to a stop sign. I happened to glance to the right and noticed a man standing on his porch in a red bandana, jeans and a t-shirt. I stopped at the stop sign then took off. I got about two blocks away, then I heard the Lord say, "Michele turn around and give that man $10.00." Readers, I could hardly turn around fast enough. I put my car in reverse and about got hit backing up as I quickly went back to this man's house. I pulled up in his driveway, got out of my car and began to tell this man how God had spoken to me and told me to give him $10.00. As I got back in my car, the man approached me slowly with both hands behind his back as a sign his intentions were not to harm me. He proceeded to ask me why I stopped to give him money. I told him because God told me to as I was just praying for God to use me. Then the man said, "I am a believer as well." We both rejoiced in God's goodness, loudly hooting and a hollering of His greatness. Then he began to suggest that I let him do something for me. I said that was not necessary, but he insisted. He gave me two phone numbers - one was a number of a Jewish lawyer and the other one was from a Greek lawyer; if I ever needed anything, they would help me out. This cracked me up. This is what he had to offer; it was suitable because of where he lived and the environment he lived in, a lawyer was priceless. This man was considered my neighbor.

We must start thinking outside our box. I can hear many of you right now saying, "Well, that was dangerous." Yes, it probably was, so make sure it is the voice of God you are hearing because the same God who asked me to stop that day was the same God who was protecting me. I made a decision to fear God more than I did people, circumstances, or my own imagination. Later on, God asked me to stop again at this man's house and I did. I learned his name was John, his mother named him after John the Baptist. We have become "drive by buddies," meaning when I drive by and he is out, we wave at each other, and occasionally when God tells me to stop and bless John, I am quick to obey.

> In Matthew 5:43-48 (NIV) says, "You have heard that it was said, 'Love your neighbor and hate your enemy.' But I tell you: Love your enemies and pray for those who persecute you, that you may be sons of your Father in heaven. He causes the sun to rise on the evil and the good, and sends rain on the righteous and the unrighteous. If you love those who love you, what reward will you get? Are not even the tax collectors doing that? And if you greet only your brothers, what are you doing more than others? Do not even pagans do that? Be perfect, therefore, as your heavenly Farther is perfect."

What makes you any different than the rest of the world except for the title "Christian?"

Over the last few months, the Lord has been using me in different ways. I have been putting together envelopes for about a year now. I pray for God to give me Scriptures, then I put money in an envelope and place them on the dash of my car and wait for God to show me who to give them to. One time, the Lord led me to the local Good Will store. He told me to go in, and He would show me to whom I would give the envelope. As I walked around the store listening for His voice, He was faithful to show me a young mother who was going to be the recipient that day. She just looked at me as if to say, "What do you want in return?" I explained that God had asked me to stop by the Good Will store and give her this gift from Him because she was on His mind today. Could fear of people have stopped me that day? Yes, but again I chose to fear God more.

Another time, I was at Wal-Mart and the Lord asked me to get out $20.00, and He would show me who to give it to. So as I was doing my grocery shopping, I was innately aware of God's presence as He led me to the woman I was to bless with this simple offering. I approached her like I had approached many before her and informed her she was on the mind of her heavenly Father and He wanted to bless her. She said, "But I don't need it." I said, "Well God wanted you to have it, so be blessed." I quickly escaped from her because I knew she was just a moment away from giving the money back. I was rushing around the store, dodging her, trying to get my shopping done as soon as possible. I was about to head down the last aisle, and as I turned the corner, there she was. She said, "Ma'am, I don't feel right about taking this money. I don't need it." I said, "God just wanted you to know you were on His mind today in a tangible way. It's okay if you don't need it for groceries. Take your children out for lunch as a special treat from God." She said, "Okay." Fearing God more than I did anything else was becoming a part of my mantra.

Another day, I was at the Dollar Store and the lady in front of me was buying a bunch of paper plates, cups, forks, spoons and knifes, along with some snacks. The cashier asked if she was getting ready for a party. She replied, "No, my father-in-law suddenly passed away, and we are having everyone over after the funeral today." Immediately, God spoke to me and said, "Pay for her purchases." After the cashier rang her up, I said, "Please allow me to pay for this for you." She said, "Are you sure?" I said, "Yes I am." She said, "Thank you so much." I said, "Not a problem." After she left, the cashier said, "There are not many people left who would have done that. As a matter of fact, I have been working here a long time and that has never happened here before." I said, "I cannot take any credit; if I was not listening to God with a fearful ear, I would have missed this opportunity myself." I left there excited about how God was using me but saddened by the cashier's voice.

Why are we as believers not making a bigger impact with our love-walk out among the people? Why have we considered our love-walk to be an option? This is the greatest command. One time last summer, I was standing in the snow cone line when a mother brought her two excited little boys to have a treat for all their hard work. I overheard her saying, "Let me make sure they accept my debit card because I don't have any cash." As she went up to the counter, her little boys were jumping with excitement over what flavor of snow cone they were going to enjoy. As their eyes began to get wider and wider with expectation, I noticed the mother returning to inform the boys the snow cone vendor did not accept debit cards. As I stood there, I slowly watched the faces of these children fall from excitement to tears as they walked back to their car. I heard the Lord say, "Buy them all a snow cone." I ran over to their car, and I asked them if they would allow me to purchase them all a snow cone. The mother was shocked but very appreciative. You know, readers, I don't know if that family believed in God or not, but what I do know is that God wanted to buy them all a snow cone that day because they were on His mind. Who am I to deny God?

Are you willing to obey God no matter what it is He is asking of you? Are you willing to love His people the way He tells you to love them? I found it interesting how each person God had asked me to bless handled His love. One was suspicious, another was jumping with joy, another did not feel worthy and still another was appreciative. How do you handle God's love?

> Matthew 22:37-39 (NIV) says, "Jesus replied, "Love the Lord your God with all your heart and with all your soul and with all your mind. This is the first and greatest commandment. And the second is like it: "Love our neighbor as yourself."

Let me ask you something, when is the last time you picked up the Word of the Lord, read it, then acted on what you read? When was the last time you were doers of the Word? When was the last time you prayed like someone was listening, lived like someone was watching, talked liked you were going to be held accountable, read the Bible like it was a manual, loved like you meant it, believed like you believed it, listened like someone was speaking? When was the last time you prayed for God to use you and meant it?

Have you ever been accused of being a radical, Bible thumping, lip smacking believer of the infallible Word of God? Or, are you unmoved by the unseen? Do you want to just read about great feats God has done, but don't want to be the one who performs them through His power. Do you say things like, "I wasn't called to be a preacher. I don't have the time others have to read the Bible." Really, what are you doing with the time you have? If you had the extra time, would you spend it reading and getting to know your Father better? Are you living a life that matters in Heaven, one that is bold with kindness, and strengthened by passion, walking as if you are walking towards something instead of away from it? I dare you to live a life for the Glory of God, to live like you mean it, to wake up all your senses. We are not living in a morgue with a bunch of dead people; we are living among the living. We are not holding a silent auction for Jesus. Why do we try to keep Him under lock and key?

Ecclesiastes 12:13-14, "Now all has been heard; here is the conclusion of the matter: Fear God and keep his command-ment, for this is the whole duty of man. For God will bring every deed into judgment, including every hidden thing, whether it is good or evil."

Fear motivates people. Don't believe me? Has anyone tried to break into your house? What motivated you to make a phone call to 911? Fear. Fear creates a space for a reaction. What about a smoker who has been smoking for 20 years and tried to quit at least 20 times, but one day they are diagnosed with cancer. Within a moment, a flash of a light, they quit smoking. Why? Fear creates a space for reaction. Someone is trying to attack you, what's the first thing you do? You react to the attack. Why? Again, fear creates a space for reaction. It's a natural instinct to react to fear. Someone hides and jumps out to scare you, you react with a scream. I believe there is a healthy fear, a fear that promotes action--an astonishing fear that inhabits our way of thinking. If your job is on the line and your boss is watching and taking notes as to who is working hard and who deserves to retain their job, does fear play a part in how you perform? Yes, it does because you don't want to lose your job.

Proverbs 1:7 says, "The fear of the Lord is the beginning of knowledge, but fools despise wisdom and discipline."

Let me propose a question--when you read the Word of the Lord, does it cause a reaction?

Choices are for the Living:

1. Do you fear God enough to obey His command to Love?

   _____
   _____
   _____
   _____
   _____
   _____
   _____
   _____
   _____
   _____
   _____
   _____

2. What does God's love look like to you? Are you satisfied with your love-walk? If not, what are some changes you can make today to improve living out the Greatest Command, "Love your neighbor as you love yourself?"

   _____
   _____
   _____
   _____
   _____
   _____
   _____
   _____
   _____
   _____
   _____
   _____

3. How are you preparing the way for Jesus?

_____
_____
_____
_____
_____
_____
_____
_____
_____
_____
_____
_____
_____

4. Do you live in a segregated world, meaning do you only
    know and hang around "Christians"? When is the last
    time you invited a non-Christian over for a meal?

_____
_____
_____
_____
_____
_____
_____
_____
_____
_____
_____
_____
_____

5. What fear motivates you? And does that fear drive you towards God or away from God?

_____
_____
_____
_____
_____
_____
_____
_____
_____
_____
_____
_____

Weekly Challenge: Go to the grocery store and ask God to show you someone to whom you can give $10.00.

Additional Notes:

_____
_____
_____
_____
_____
_____
_____
_____
_____
_____
_____
_____

Chapter 5

You're Just Not Into Him That Much...

Mark 10:21, "Jesus looked at him and loved him. 'One thing you lack,' he said, 'Go, sell everything you have and give to the poor, and you will have treasure in heaven. Then come, follow me.'"

$\mathcal{J}$ watched an Oprah show a few years back. She had a male guest on who was willing to expose men's secrets about dating. They eventually made a movie based off the episode, but the point of the show was to flash a light on the secrets of men and why some tell the lies they tell. As her guest started to explain the motives of men, Oprah allowed him to take some questions from the audience which I found fascinating. The first lady stood up and asked, "Why does a guy tell you he will call you after the first date but never does?" The man's response was shocking and brutally honest, "He's just not into you that much." At the end of the night, he tells you what you want to hear so he can escape quietly into the sunset of his own deception as he rides off on his black horse. That comment made me stop and think about our relationship with God. Do we call on every name but the name of our God? When we get into a financial situation, do we call on the name of the banker? When we have trouble disciplining our kids, do we call on a friend for advice? When we are having marriage troubles, do we call on the name of a counselor? I'm not saying we can't utilize our resources; all I'm saying is, shouldn't we first be seeking God? Shouldn't we be into Him that much? It is deceiving ourselves to pretend like we trust God, but depend on everything but Him.

The next lady stood up and asked, "If a guy has been dating you for several years but is not willing to put a ring on your finger, what does that mean?" Again, the guest of the show said, "He is just not into you that much." I was shocked again by his reply but realized the truth in his transparency. I thought about how, in essence, we do the same thing to God. We hang out with Him at church on Sunday, maybe even open our Bible on Monday, but other than a few glances His way, we are not really sold out, on fire, loaded with excitement to be in His presence. Why? Maybe, we are not into Him that much.

As the third lady stood up, she asked, "What if a guy only dates you in secret?" He never takes you out in public; he never introduces you to his friends or his family, he only wants to be around you at his place behind closed doors. Once again, Oprah's guest replied with the same answer, "He's just not into you that much." Once more, I had to ponder his answer and compare it to the way we treat our Lord and Savior. When is the last time you introduced your Lord to someone or brought His name up to your non-believing family, or to a co-worker? Are you into Him that much? I believe the underlying problem in it all is we simply do not fear the Lord of the universe. We play way too many instruments with our Lord, and we act like a one man band, when all He wanted was the instrument of our obedience.

Elijah was a man who obeyed the Lord because he knew the God he served; he knew of His power, he was sure of the outcome. If God told him to do it, that was good enough. Oh no, not us. We want to seek 10 people, fast, pray, fast again, seek 3 more people, and then, if we do it at all, we do it with doubt and unbelief in our hearts and wonder why there was no success story to our obedience.

Elijah was a prophet whom God sent to Israel and Judah. Israel had fallen morally and spiritually. God had sent many prophets to no avail. The kings ignored the prophets and continued to lead the people into idolatry. There were very few priests left from the tribe of Levi. The priest had become corrupt along with the kings; there was no one left to bring God's Word forth. No one appeared to fear the Lord. They had been worshipping Baal, the god who they believed brought the rain and a bountiful harvest. But one day, the Lord found someone who apparently feared Him enough to obey Him.

> The Lord spoke to Elijah and told him to make an announcement against their rain god, Baal. "Now Elijah the Tishbite, from Tishbe in Gilead, said to Ahab, 'As the Lord, and the God of Israel, lives, whom I serve, there will be neither dew nor rain in the next few years except at my word.' Then the word of the Lord came to Elijah, 'Leave here, turn eastward and hide in Kerith Ravine, east of Jordan. You will drink from the brook, and I have ordered the ravens to feed you there.' So he did what the Lord had told him. He went to the Kerith Ravine, east of the Jordan, and stayed there. The ravens brought him bread and meat in the morning and bread and meat in the evening, and he drank from the brook (1Kings 17:1–6)."

When we fear the Lord enough to do what He is asking us to do, there is an awakening of knowledge. If we never attempt to do what the Lord our God is telling us to do, how will we ever understand what lies behind the command? I'm sure Elijah had no idea what lay ahead on the journey he was taking. "Praise the Lord! Blessed is the man who fears the Lord, who finds great delight in his commands" (Psalm 112:1). "The fear of the Lord is the beginning of knowledge" (Proverbs 1:7). So this tells me, without the fear of the Lord there is no beginning of knowledge. Well, that explains some things. This might be why so many of the Lord's people are walking around perishing because the Word of the Lord says, "My people perish from lack of knowledge" (Hosea 4:6). Their dreams are perishing, their hopes are perishing, and their aspirations are perishing. If I were to interpret the above Scriptures, it would look something like this: When we clothe ourselves with the fear of the Lord, we are dressing ourselves in a non-perishable suit of obedient fragrance which God Himself has orchestrated for our success in advance.

Elijah has just popped up on the scene. This is the first time we have heard of him, and he announces there will be a drought. He tells King Ahab the rain god you think is so powerful is a wimp. He is nothing but a figment of your imagination. He has no power and no authority to bring rain or prevent rain from coming. Now the God I serve has filled my words with power. Not only will it rain when I say, but I will rest beside a stream of water while your crops wither up and die. My God will feed me a meatloaf sandwich with the feet of a raven by day, and by night, I will feast on a buffet of meat with a side of bread. My God, the God I serve, will keep me safe under the sky of His protection. The field I rest my body upon will be His grace and the earth's blanket will cover me with peace. Are you into your God that much? Would you speak such a statement with the confidence of Elijah?

Some time had passed and the Lord spoke to Elijah again. The brook had dried up, and God told him to pack his bags, go to Zarephath and stay there. God said I have spoken to a widow, not just any widow, but a widow I know by the Spirit will supply you with food. Let's see what Elijah unpacks from his bag. 1 Kings 17: 10-13 (NIV), "So he went to Zarephath. When he came to the town gate, a widow was there gathering sticks. He called to her and asked, 'Would you bring me a little water in a jar so that I may have a drink?' As she was going to get it, he called, 'And bring me, please, a piece of bread.' 'As surely as the Lord your God lives,' she replied, 'I don't have any bread - only a handful of flour in a jar and a little oil in a jug. I am gathering a few sticks to take home and make a meal for myself and my son, that we may eat it - and die.' Elijah said to her, 'Don't be afraid, go home and do as you have said."

What is the first thing Elijah told the widow? "Don't be afraid." Remember what I said in the beginning of the book? There are two different kinds of fear: "So do not fear for I am with you" (Isaiah 41:10a). And, "By faith Noah, when warned about things not yet seen, in holy fear built an ark to save his family" (Hebrews 11:7). Here is a great illustration of what can be accomplished in the natural realm if we are willing to let the spiritual realm guide us on our journey on a fearless walk with God -

One day I went to our local Recreation Center where we are members. I worked out as I normally do, then I went inside the sauna. For the last several months, the Lord has been using me to witness to the unsaved. It all started when I challenged my Monday night Bible class to challenge themselves to do something that is not comfortable, to step out in faith and do what God tells them to do no matter how it looks. My challenge to myself was to witness to someone by just asking if they knew Jesus. Although I had witnessed to many people on many occasions, I had never just out right asked someone if they knew Jesus.

The first time this happened, I was sitting in the sauna. I felt like the Lord said, "Ask the man who is in here with you." I did as the Lord had asked, and the man answered my question with a yes. "Awesome!," I said, then we had a fantastic conversation about how good God is. Then next time I went to the gym, the same thing happened. The person answered "yes" to my question about if they knew Jesus. Again, the hot sauna was filled with praises to the Lord. But then there was this day, a day unlike any other day, a day that would be etched into my mind forever. The memory will never escape or be too far from my thoughts. I worked out like all the days before, then I proceeded to the sauna, which by the way, is a great witnessing place. The heat portrays hell well, so it's a constant reminder of the importance of being a witness for Jesus. I walked in and there was only one little man, who looked like he could be a horse jockey, sitting at the left top of the sauna. I sat down, and within moments, I felt the Lord nudging me to share His Son with this man.

We began to talk, and as he began to share his life with me, he started telling me about his daughter and how she lives with his mother, and his ex-wife was a drug addict and no longer has anything to do with the daughter. He said his daughter went to church and was active in the youth. I thought to myself, "Okay, here's my gate into this man's life." I asked, "Where do you go to church?" He said, "I don't." He went on to say, "My daughter is studying to become a youth pastor." I replied, "You must be so proud." He said, "No, I wish she would find something else to do." I said, "Oh." Then he went on to explain the conversation he and his daughter always ended up having when they visit--she wants to know why he doesn't believe in God and he wants to know why she does?

Readers, it was as if God Himself opened my mouth and poured His words out of me. I felt the power of Jesus resonating throughout my body, or that might have been fear. Before I could blink an eye, my mouth was open, and I must admit, I was battling with fear. I looked up at him and said these words, "Mister you know what I would say if you asked me that question?" and before he could answer, I proceeded to tell him, "Look, if I'm wrong, I will have lived a good life putting others first. Then if I died, I would be buried six foot under. But if you're wrong, you will be burning in a fiery hell for eternity." His eyes drew a blank, and he bolted for the door. I thought he was going to punch me or pass out. He was furious. I have never done that before, never in that way, never in that sauna, but I will tell you this, I believe with all that's in me I was an answer to his daughter's prayers that day in the fiery sauna. I did not dress my words in cotton fluff up with fabric softener. I let them leave my mouth as they entered, and by the power of God, they pierced the soul of a man. I pray the man I witnessed to finds the heart of Jesus. I have never seen him again, but if I do, I will speak whatever God tells me to speak. Who knows, I might get to walk him through the salvation prayer one day at the Recreation Center...if he ever comes back. If we all walked in the fear of the Lord, could you imagine the possibilities?

Now let's see what else Elijah told this widow women. In I Kings 17:13, "Don't be afraid, Go!" The word "Go" is written 1,487 times in the Bible. The Great Commission says, "Go!" Every miracle begins with an act of obedience; it begins with go. Naaman was told to go dip himself in the dirty Jordan. Jesus said to the lame man, "Pick up your mat and go." The ten lepers were told to go show themselves to the priest, and while they were going, they were healed. Can I tell you something? Some of you are waiting on your miracle; you are waiting on what you've been standing on the Word of God for. What you have cried yourself to sleep about. What you have prayed for in secret. The answer is in the going. I do not have the time to exhaust all 1,487 times the Bible says the word "Go," but it says it enough to grab my attention and it should grab yours. In the book of Luke, fourth chapter verses 25 through 26 it says, "I assure you that there were many widows in Israel in Elijah's time, when the sky was shut for three and a half years and there was a severe famine throughout the land. Yet Elijah was not sent to any of them, but to a widow in Zarephath."

Have you ever asked yourself why Elijah was sent to this particular widow, in this particular town? Well, I did, and I believe the answer is found in First Timothy, fifth chapter fifth verse, it says, "The widow who is really in need and left all alone puts her faith and hope in God and continues night and day to pray and to ask God for help." This was the Mosaic Law. The widow was seeking God for help, and God spoke to Elijah. Elijah was into God that much that he listened and obeyed. Elijah was willing to be an answer to her prayers, and because Elijah was willing, God used him. Elijah was living Matthew 25:35-46, which I discussed in detail in chapter one. **"The fear of the Lord is the beginning of knowledge" (Proverbs 1:7).** Elijah was building his own ark to save a dying women and her child. The last thing Elijah told the widow women was "do!" Elijah said to her in 1Kings 17:13-14, "Don't be afraid, Go home, and Do as you have said. But first make a small cake of bread for me from what you have and bring it to me, and then make something for yourself and your son."

Elijah is telling her do whatever you're planning on doing, but first serve me, then yourself. Wow! Remember when I said every miracle starts with going? Well, Elijah is telling her do whatever you need to do, but first "go" and make me a small cake of bread. The widow women did what Elijah told her to do and there was enough food for about two and a half years. The jar of flour was not used up and the jug of oil did not run dry in keeping with the Word of the Lord spoken by Elijah.[19] When Elijah answered the call to be an answer to the widow women's prayer, he didn't know at the time, his willingness would be an answer to many prayers.

For example, let's look at *Jonah 1:1, "The word of the Lord came to*

Jonah son of Amittai." Amittai is believed to have been the husband of the widow women whom Elijah helped. Her son, who Elijah laid on and God revived in 1Kings 17:19-22, is believed by many scholars and Jewish traditions to be Jonah. In Jonah chapter 4, Jonah ended up preaching in the streets of Nineveh, the most important city in Assyria. The people repented and 120,000 people were saved. All because Elijah was willing to hear the voice of God and obey; he was willing to be an answer to somebody else's prayer. Now, let's say just for argument's sake, that Amittai was not the husband of the widow women, and therefore, Jonah was not the boy who Elijah laid on and God brought back to life[20]. It still does not alter the fact that lives were changed. A women and her son were saved from death. Elijah obeyed God and miracles happened. Elijah was a man who was into God that much.

Choices are for the Living:

1. Are you into Him that much? When was the last time you heard the voice of God and obeyed?

_____
_____
_____
_____
_____
_____
_____
_____
_____
_____
_____
_____

2. When was the last time you did something outrageous for your God that required you to put the fear of man aside and fear God? Explain how you felt in that moment when you decided to go for it.

_____
_____
_____
_____
_____
_____
_____
_____
_____
_____
_____
_____

3. If you were the widow women in this story, what do you think might have been your reply when Elijah told her to go make him something to eat first?

_____
_____
_____
_____
_____
_____
_____
_____
_____
_____
_____
_____

4. Who and what do you run to when you need help? What name do you call on?

_____
_____
_____
_____
_____
_____
_____
_____
_____
_____
_____
_____

5. Are you willing to be an answer to someone else's prayer today?

_____
_____
_____
_____
_____
_____
_____
_____
_____
_____
_____
_____

Weekly Challenge: Ask a stranger if they know Jesus.

Additional Notes:

_____
_____
_____
_____
_____
_____
_____
_____
_____
_____
_____
_____
_____

Chapter 6

Until I Can Learn What God Will Do For Me

1 Samuel 22:3, "...until I learn what God will do for me"

*I*n 1 Samuel 22:1-5, "David left Gath and escaped to the cave of Adullam. When his brothers and his father's household heard about it, they went down to him there. All those who were in distress or in debt or discontented gathered around him, and he became their leader. About four hundred men were with him. From there David went to Mizpah in Moab and said to the king of Moab, 'Would you let my father and mother come and stay with you **until I learn what God will do for me?'** So he left them with the king of Moab, and they stayed with him as long as David was in the stronghold. But the prophet Gad said to David, 'Do not stay in the stronghold, Go into the land of Judah.' So David left and went to the forest of Hereth."

As I was reading the Scriptures, I noticed a few interesting statements that David made. For example, "Would you let my father and mother come stay with you **until I learn what God will do for me**." How quickly David had forgotten what God had done for him. Remember when David was sent by his father to feed his brothers who were on the battle line in 1 Samuel 17? David was the youngest, and small in stature, so he was not allowed to fight alongside his brothers, only to bring them food. David approached them as they were discussing how the king would give great wealth to the man who kills Goliath. In addition, the king would give his daughter in marriage and would exempt the man's father's family from taxes in Israel. In 1 Samuel 17:26, "David asked the men standing near him, 'What will be done for the man who kills this Philistine and removes this disgrace from Israel?'" 1 Samuel 17:27 says, "They repeated to him what they had been saying and told him, 'This is what will be done for the man who kills him.'"

When David asked them to repeat what they said, I had to laugh. I thought to myself, "Was David not listening when they said it the first time?" Maybe this explains why David made the comment, **"I need to learn what God will do for me."** Readers, David said this after he had defended himself to Saul as to why he thought he should be allowed to fight the giant, Goliath. David presented Saul with his résumé. He said, "I have been keeping my father's sheep. When a lion or bear came and carried off a sheep from the flock, I went after it, struck it and rescued the sheep from its mouth. When it turned on me, I seized it by its hair, struck it and killed it." Then David went on to say in 1 Samuel 17:37, "The Lord who delivered me from the paw of the lion and the paw of the bear will deliver me from the hand of this Philistine." Then with a sling shot and a stone, David killed the giant, Goliath.

It is like David had spiritual amnesia. Just a few chapters before, David was naming off a laundry list of things God had done for him. Now, he was saying **I need to learn what God will do for me.**

Throughout my life, God has shown Himself in incredible ways. Each time God showed up to rescue me out of the paw of the lion, I allowed each situation to build my faith to a higher level. "I will remember the deeds of the Lord; yes, I will remember your miracles of long ago. I will meditate on all your works and consider all your mighty deeds" (Psalm 77:11-12). This verse is the meditation of my heart. I call the challenges in my life "faith builders." We better know what God will do for us. We better know what His Word says. We better know what our birthrights consist of, or else we might be the sheep that gets stuck in the lion's paw, looking for David, instead of counting on God. If we don't know who we are in Christ, we will become someone we were never meant to be.

The other thing I noticed after David inquired, **"what God would do for him,"** was the comment the prophet Gad said to David, "Do not stay in the stronghold, Go into the land of Judah." Gad was warning David. He was saying, "Listen, get out of this stronghold and go into the land of Judah." Too many of God's saints strap themselves into the stronghold of life; they give in, give up, and give out just before their miracle. I looked up what the name "Judah" meant in Hebrew. It means *"to praise."* Wow! Gad was not only telling David to get out of the stronghold, but he was telling him how to get out. He was telling David to go to the land of praise (Judah) and start praising.

Some of you need to start praising your God for your victory. Stop saying, like David, **"I need to learn what God will do for me."** Rest on what God has already done for you. Praise Him like you mean it, praise Him like you believe it and praise Him like you know Him. Stop pretending like you can draw how big God is on the size of paper you're comfortable drawing on. Some of us have drawn God with little distinction between Him and us. Trust me, our view has been skewed for entirely too long.

This is what our drawing might look like...

But in reality He is the God of the Universe who holds up the entire world with His spoken Word.

Many of you still haven't learned what God will do for you. Countless of you reading this book right now don't even know these seven promises God made specifically to mankind, which means you and me.

1. He has promised to supply every need we have - Philippians 4:19.

2. God has promised that His grace is sufficient for us - II Corinthians 12:9.

3. God has promised us victory over death. He first resurrected Jesus as a way of assuring our resurrection. Peter said: "This Jesus hath God raised up, whereof we are all witnesses" Acts 2:32.

4. God has promised that all things work together for good to those who love and serve Him faithfully - Romans 8:28.

5. God has promised that those who believe in Jesus and are baptized for the forgiveness of sins will be saved - Mark 16:16 and Acts 2:38.

6. We will not be overtaken by temptation. God is faithful; he will not let you be tempted beyond what you can bear - 1 Corinthians 10:13.

7. God has promised His people eternal life - John 10:27-28.

Readers, we need to get a fresh revelation on what God will do for us, believe it, act on it and remember it.

It was evident that David wanted to impress his God. He bragged on Him often, even if he did suffer from temporary amnesia from time to time. This made me think...when we were children, didn't we want to impress our dad? Whether it was with a good report card, a good job mowing the lawn or helping around the house, didn't a part of you just want to hear, "Good job, son" or "Good job, daughter?" Now that you are all grown up, do you still want to hear those words? What about from your Heavenly Father? Do we even care if the Lord thinks we are doing a good job or are we just in a habit of living our lives to hear the praises of men? We don't obey for the reward, but our reward will be in proportion to our fear of God.

How many of you grew up in a household that when you got into trouble, you could hear the belt slipping through the belt loops of your dad's pants? And in that moment, there was fear, real unsolicited fear? Well, it may have been solicited by the way you behaved. What about now? What are some of the consequences you have for your kids when they choose not to obey? Do you take their cell phone away if they use up too many minutes? Do your younger children get an old fashioned spanking if they talk back to you? What about when your teenage driver stays out past curfew? Do you take the keys for a while? I had a vision one day--what if God disciplined us the way we discipline our children when they disobey?

Imagine talking on your cell phone one day and God told you to pray for the person on the other line. You chose to ignore His request and kept right on talking. In the middle of your conversation, the Lord grabbed your cell phone and took it to Heaven. How about if the Lord said, "I want you to go ask _____ for forgiveness," and you said, "No! I think they need to ask me for forgiveness! It's their turn this time, Lord, I always apologize first." Just as the words left your mouth, you hear the belt going through the belt loops of God's pants. And right then and there, wherever you were standing, the Lord starts wearing your bottom out all the way to Heaven.

Here's another scenario: you're driving down the road singing your praise music, while lifting your holy hands. As you come to a red light, your eyes catch a glimpse of a homeless man holding a sign reading, "Hungry; please help!" The Lord taps you on the arm, the same one that was lifted to praise His name, and whispers in your ear. Yes, the same ear you were absorbing the praise music with. You hear Him say, "Go buy this man a cheeseburger." You don't say a word. The Lord repeats His request, "Go buy this man a cheeseburger." You think about it, then you say, "Lord I am in a hurry. Someone else will buy him a cheeseburger. He needs to get a job, anyway. He's not my responsibility." As the light turns green, suddenly God yanks the keys out of your ignition and takes them to Heaven where He puts them in a safe place; your car is no longer of any use to you. Then you heard those dreaded words, "You are grounded."

This is fun! Let's look at another possibility. It is Sunday morning, and everyone is rushing around getting ready for church. Mom is making sure the younger kids are getting dressed, brushing their teeth and finding their shoes. While the older ones are fighting, I mean "discussing," who's wearing whose clothes or who has been in the other one's room using their perfume, hairspray, and make-up, all while the dogs are begging to go outside. The clock strikes eight times and everyone in the house knows it's time to get in the car. As the family heads out, one of the children look over in the corner and there sits dad. He looks up and says, "Looks like we are going to be late again. I was rude to mom and God put me in another time out."

For many of us, we don't fear God because we don't think there will be any consequences for our sins. Have we conveniently forgotten about Judgment Day? I heard someone say, "You can choose your sin but you can't choose your consequence." Revelation 20:11-14 (NIV), "Then I saw a great white throne and him who was seated on it. Earth and sky fled from his presence, and there was no place for them. And I saw the dead, great and small, standing before the throne, and books were opened. Another book was opened, which is the book of life. The dead were judged according to what they had done as recorded in the books. The sea gave up the dead that were in it, and death and Hades gave up the dead that were in them, and each person was judged according to what he had done."

Have we become tone-deaf? Can we no longer hear the tone in God's voice when He asks us to do something? Do we think He is saying pray; when He's really saying $\mathrm{PRAY?}$ When we read in Galatians 5:14, "The entire law is summed up in a single command: "Love your neighbor as yourself." Are we hearing love, when God is saying $\mathrm{LOVE?}$ If we, as Christians, could master these two things, it would change the world around us for eternity. Have we become deaf to His tone? Do you know what God will do for you?

Choices are for the Living:

1. If you could draw God, would you have a piece of paper big enough to express His image? Write down your image of God, His attributes, His traits, His character. Do you live like you believe in the character of God?

    _____
    _____
    _____
    _____
    _____
    _____
    _____
    _____
    _____
    _____
    _____
    _____
    _____

2. Are you confident in what the Lord will do for you? Discuss the last time you had real confidence in the God you serve. What drew you to that confidence? Memorize Psalm 77:11-12.

    _____
    _____
    _____
    _____
    _____
    _____
    _____
    _____
    _____
    _____
    _____
    _____

3. Would your life look different if you feared the Lord more than man? If so, how? What would you do for the kingdom of God if fear was not a factor? Today commit to doing at least one thing on your list that you are afraid to do.

_____
_____
_____
_____
_____
_____
_____
_____
_____
_____
_____
_____

4. What promise are you standing on right now for your life?

_____
_____
_____
_____
_____
_____
_____
_____
_____
_____
_____
_____

5. Write down whatever promises you are standing on. In addition, write down the answered promise, along with the day and time the promise comes to pass--when God shows Himself faithful. It will become one of your faith builders in the future.

_____
_____
_____
_____
_____
_____
_____
_____
_____
_____
_____
_____
_____

Weekly Challenge: Volunteer at your local homeless shelter. Write about your experience.

Additional Notes:

_____
_____
_____
_____
_____
_____
_____
_____
_____
_____
_____
_____
_____

Chapter 7

It's Not About Me...Or Is It?

Matthew 6:33 "But seek first His kingdom....."

*Matthew 6:33, "But seek first His kingdom and His righ-
teousness, and all the things will be given to you as well."*

First - is the Greek word "proton," meaning "firstly in time,
place, order, or importance." Simply put, it means before
anything else, before what you've planned with your time, before
your husband, wife, kids, parents, friends, church, job, house and
entertainment. First means before. We just need to love Him more
than anything else. We might need to step back and critique our
motives for serving Him. We may need to reevaluate what is really
important to His kingdom. Then we may need to ask ourselves one
question, is what God says important, important to us? **What is
God's kingdom? What does God want us to seek? What does
seeking His righteousness look like?**

Have you ever really pondered this passage or did you assume
you've already grasped the wisdom behind the teaching? How far
did you dig to get your wisdom? I am going to make an attempt
to examine these questions and give you my honest opinion, but
I encourage you to pull out the scrolls of God's written Word and
investigate the meaning for yourself by meditating on His Word.

Seek - is the Greek word "zelos," it describes "a fierce
determination to have something or to become something, a
constant and arduous seeking to obtain something, not just an
occasional attempt.[22]" After reading the definitions, I quickly
realized how short I fall in seeking my God first. According to the
Greek definition of the word "first," it means putting God first in
time, place and importance. If the body of Christ would be brutally
honest with ourselves, we would realize, as far as importance
goes, we have scaled God so far back that many of us haven't even
thought about where God is in the pecking order of our lives. Isaiah
29:13 (NIV), "The Lord says, 'These people come near me with their
mouths and honor me with their lips, but their hearts are far from
me. Their worship of me is made up only of rules taught by men.'"

Wow! When did we hand over God's power to men? Many of
us worship when we're told and stop when we are told, but did
you know you can worship God outside of the Sunday service?
Yes, that's right! You can praise and worship God whenever your
heart desires, and therein lies the problem. Many of us don't get
into worship that much. We have to be led like a seeing eye dog

leads his owner. Many of us are blind to the importance of worship. Therefore, instead of grabbing our walking stick, we remain seated, stagnant, stale and in a slumber. How far have we strayed from first seeking the kingdom of God?

In the above paragraph, I asked **"What is the Kingdom of God?"** I believe the Kingdom of God is Heaven and earth, all that He made, which is filled with His people. Who has ever had a kingdom with no one in the kingdom? Have we reduced ourselves to lip service? Have we been whispering sweet nothings in God's ear? Do we tell Him we want to be used, but when He gives us an assignment, we politely decline the invitation because it may be cleaning the church toilets, making someone a meal, mowing someone's lawn or feeding the hungry? Have we become con artists with Christ? Do we try to con Him into our way of thinking, our way of living or our way of loving? 1 John 3:18 (NIV) says, "Dear children, let us not love with words or tongue but with actions and in truth."

Come on body of Christ, just as we represent our parents when we are out and about, we also represent our God. When your church asks for volunteers to help serve the body, where is your name on the signup sheet? Do you pass the clip board with the attitude, "I always sign up," or do you say things like, "I'll let someone else do it"? It's okay not to write your name down if God tells you not to. I've withheld my name on the clip board on several occasions, but just make sure you're not serving Him a "word sandwich." Let's put some action behind the baloney we're so comfortable giving Him. What if someone asked you to make them a glass of water and you agreed. As they sat there waiting for their water, you cleaned a bathroom, answered a phone call, read a couple of chapters in a book, took the dog on a walk and then went out to eat. Did you serve them? Yes, you served them your lip service. This is what God means when we come near Him with our mouth and honor Him with our lips but our hearts are far from Him.

Are you comfortable lip syncing? Have ever seen someone lip sync when the words aren't matching? It's painful to watch, a little awkward. It's like I'm watching a fake performance, and I wonder if this is how God feels sometimes when our words have become more important than our actions? I wonder if God feels like He's watching a fake performance while we lip sync love songs to our imaginary God. We sing, "Oh how I love you," but do we? And if we do, how much do we love Him? Sometimes we try to reconstruct God with our own thoughts, and then we give praise to what we think. We boldly stand on what we believe, on what we consider to be the truth. We have inflated our opinions with the helium of this world, but eventually the balloon deflates. Our opinions begin to fade into the backdrop of destruction, because our houses are being built on sand.

There is only one infallible, un-deflectable Word of God, the Bible. Even this book you're reading is based off my opinion with the exception of the Scriptures. Travel lightly on the words of men, but put every bit of your weight on the Word of God.

Do we love Him enough to first, before anything or anyone else, seek His kingdom? **"What does God want us to seek?"** Seek Him with a fierce determination, to have Him at all costs, a constant seeking to obtain, not an occasional attempt. Do we love Him enough for it not to be about us? Do we love Him enough to take Him at His word? Remember fear creates a space for re-action? Proverbs 1:7, "The fear of the Lord is the beginning of knowledge." Jesus Himself knew how to seek with a fierce determination to have us at all costs. Luke 19:10 says, "For the Son of Man came to seek and to save what was lost." Do we love God enough to seek what is lost? I think what is lost is our passion to seek God and His Kingdom. Do we seek Him with fierce determination? To have Him at all costs? What does that even look like to you? How much are we willing to give up to obtain an authentic relationship with our Lord?

I can hear the readers now say, "It's easier said than done." For those of you who are thinking this, you are absolutely right, but God did not say seek everything that is easy to seek, seek my Kingdom with a ho-hum attitude or seek until you feel like hiding. He didn't say do everything you want to do first and whatever time you have left, your scraps, offer to Me. And if you don't have any time on some days, then that's okay; it's all about you and the kingdom your building anyway. I'll be here waiting, knocking at your door, anticipating your footsteps in the foyer. What do we need to do to seek His kingdom first? Luke 9:23, "If anyone would come after me, he must deny himself and take up his cross daily and follow me."

Mark 15:15-20, "Wanting to satisfy the crowd, Pilate released Barabbas to them. He had Jesus flogged, and handed Him over to be crucified. The soldiers led Jesus away into the palace (that is, the Praetorium) and called together the whole company of soldiers. They put a purple robe on Him, then twisted together a crown of thorns and set it on Him. And they began to call out to Him, 'Hail, king of the Jews!' Again and again they struck Him on the head with a staff and spit on Him. Falling on their knees, they paid homage to Him. And when they had mocked Him, they took off the purple robe and put His own clothes on Him. Then they led Him out to crucify Him."

Wow! Did you notice everything about Jesus' crucifixion was about His flesh? They crucified His flesh, and they gave His flesh "40 lashes minus one," known as flogging, which was a horrible punishment (see Deuteronomy 25:1 – 3). They flogged Jesus so bad that His flesh was shredded, His intestines were exposed. They had beaten Him almost unto death. He was saturated in His own blood, then everyone spit on Him until He was dripping with saliva. They put a purple robe on Him, along with a crown of thorns which was thrust into His skull. As the robe began to stick to His mutilated skin, the blood began to dry. His wounds were shrinking back into a clotting position where healing may have begun, but suddenly, they pulled the purple robe off, re-opening His wounds and exposing His flesh. He stood there while they dressed Him back into His own clothes and led Him away to be nailed to a cross where every drop of His blood spilled from His body for us.

Our flesh wants to do whatever it wants. We don't want to submit, to give all we have, to be sold out for Jesus, because our flesh has only received "two lashes minus one." We have only allowed a spiritual spanking with a feather, the thorns in our crown are made of cotton balls, the nails in our hands and feet are nothing but string beans. What have we really given up? What has it really cost us as believers in America?

Jesus is telling us in Luke 9, in order to follow Him, our flesh must be crucified daily. I noticed Jesus' flesh took the beatings. Jesus' flesh took the nails in the hand. Jesus' flesh took the crown made of thorns. Jesus' flesh was spit upon. Our flesh must die in order to do God's will. Many of us think, "I will serve God later." We think of the kingdom of Heaven as a far off place, but we don't know when the numbers of our days will expire. Many people died today thinking they had tomorrow. Some of you are in the habit of preparing for your life on earth and taking no consideration that this is a temporary home. James 4:14 says, "Why, you don't even know what will happen tomorrow. What is your life? You are a mist that appears for a little while and then vanishes."

When I share what God is calling me to do, I have so many people comment, "Well I don't feel like God is calling me to do that." I understand God might not be calling you to do exactly what I am doing, but I assure you He is calling you to do something. It is far easier to make up excuses than to actually do the will of God. But one day, you and I will stand before the Lord and give an account for what we did and didn't do here on earth. I pray I never become complacent doing the will of God before I vanish. I pray I never forget the 118 times the Bible demands me to fear my God, because in the fear comes knowledge.

I would like to give some breath to my words, a living testimony of how we can pick up our cross, deny the flesh and follow Him... because it's not about us.

I had a lady in my class named Allison. She is living a life worth repeating. Allison has a ministry called "Beauticians on a Mission." Her focus is to give back to others in need through a variety of outreach programs. She has served in the Kansas City soup kitchen, Olathe food pantry, and the Hope House for girls. Right now, she is taking donations for her "Backpack Mission" here in Kansas City which she fills with helpful items like socks, hats, t-shirts, blankets, gloves, washcloths, Band-Aids, combs, etc... Then she gathers some people, and they distribute the filled backpacks with their best efforts to serve the homeless. Allison has figured out her life is not really about her at all, but about the kingdom of God.

There is something I haven't told you about Allison. On her journey to discovering that it's not about her, she had to live a life that was. Allison had to see herself in a mirror and realize the reflection she wanted to see was Jesus, but instead, the reflection she saw was a broken, beat-down woman who was searching for something that had never been lost.

For as long as Allison could remember, she wanted to be loved by a boy. The day finally arrived. She met "G." and propelled into one of her first storms. She knew his standards were not like hers. Allison knew they were not compatible at all. She was raised with the values of a Christian home, and he was not. He got into trouble with the law several times, but she chose to ignore that rebellious side of him. She was sixteen and in love. She found herself giving him a part of her which she wished she could have saved for marriage. Over time, he became verbally abusive. He said and did things that are far better off left unspoken. "G." and Allison were married. Then, the abuse intensified and finally escalated from verbal to physical in one fell swoop of his hand. As Allison lay prostrate on the floor, she was in shock. Allison left "G." and decided to take a breath.

Still embedded with the pain of her past, she closed her eyes and held onto her dream of finding a man who would love her. As she turned to take a breath, she inhaled and met "R." But it wasn't long before she realized she had gotten involved with yet another man who was not the man she dreamed he would be. He was into pornography, lies and deceit. She suddenly found herself trying to etch out a piece of acceptance from someone who could never accept her the way she desired to be accepted. Allison was looking for her healing in another human being, and because no one could heal her but God, they all fell short of fulfilling her need for deliverance.

Early in the relationship, she found out she was pregnant. With no regrets of her pregnancy, she stayed with "R." and held onto hope. She never let go of hope, even if her hope was aimed horizontally when it should have been headed vertically. Hope is an interesting word. It means "a feeling of expectation and desire for a certain thing to happen." Allison expected to actually experience a healthy relationship. She expected to experience true love, but what was true love? How would she know if she was experiencing it if she had never felt it before?

Nine years elapsed. Allison had three kids and found herself facing yet another storm in her life, but she still had hope. Although she was still expecting, the measure of expectancy had begun to diminish as she watched her marriage dissolve right before her eyes. "R." wanted out. Allison started to find her hope vertically as she began to pray to her God, pleading with Him to see her through this desperate moment in her life. She found her emotions running through the field of her mind like a pack of wild dogs running through the streets of the night, rummaging through trash cans,

Michele Davenport

disturbing the peace as solace has dissipated. She couldn't contain the pain of another failed relationship. She had been betrayed in every way. It was in this moment she chose to stop the abuse, starting with her. She chose to begin to look at her God in a vertical fashion.

As God swooped up Allison in His arms, as He does with His children at times, she began to feel her healing. She began to exhale a sigh of relief because she knew she was given another chance to inhale the breath of His Word as it washed over her, cleansing her and making her whole. She woke up one morning as God was whispering to her the verses from 1 Peter 2: 21-25, "For to this you were called because Christ also suffered for us, leaving us an example, that you should follow His steps: 'who committed no sin, nor was deceit found in His mouth,' who when He was reviled, did not revile in return; when He suffered He did not threaten, but committed Himself to Him who judges righteously; who Himself bore our sins in His own body on the tree, that we, having died to sins, might live for righteousness by whose stripes you were healed. For you were like a sheep going astray, but have now returned to the shepherd and over seer of your soul." After the revelation of the Word nailed itself to her heart, she realized God was going to use her pain for His Glory. She was going to be a living testimony of His forgiveness extended to others on levels she has not obtained yet, but is still striving for daily. She's still discovering God's honest, patient, and unconditional love for her as she explores the serenity of God's presence.

Even though Allison's story has been one of trials and tribulations, she is willing to listen and obey the voice of God. She has allowed her healing to escort her into the arms of obedience. Allison's life is a beautiful example of loving others as you would yourself. Although she has endured many storms in her life, she refuses to ignore the hurting people around her. It's interesting to ponder what comes natural for us to do right after a huge storm. Most of us go and take inventory of the damage, but Allison took inventory of what she had learned through it all. She let God sharpen the rough edges of her life to reveal His faithfulness through her storms. She could have chosen to continue to take inventory of the pain she endured through those years of refining, but not Allison. She has learned the art of seeking Him first...not a guy, not a house, not a job, not the materialism of this world, but the realism of the spiritual kingdom she has not yet seen. Allison has chosen to pick up her cross, seek her God with a fierce determination, while remembering her life was never meant to be about her, but about others. Allison takes God at His Word, lives by Matthew 25: 34-46 and trembles at God's Word. Allison is fully aware of the excuses she had not to serve God, but realizes all the excuses in the world would never have been enough to cover disobedience to Jesus who obeyed unto death so she might live.[23] Allison is now happily married to a man who adores her, who found her, as she found an authentic relationship with her Creator.

The Greatest command is love. The conclusion is this: Grace and Truth are your outer wear for your inner healing. Adorn yourself with Jesus and allow forgiveness to be a necessity you wear every day as you put on your garment of praise.

As I was listening to a radio station the other day, I caught a young girl talking about how she has purposed herself every day to do something kind for someone else. This is what it's about, readers. "So in everything, do to others what you would have them do to you, for this sums up the Law and the Prophets" (Matthew 7:12 NIV).

If you were homeless, would you want someone to care? Would you want someone to notice, to glance your way with eyes of compassion? If you were cold, would you want someone to give you a blanket? If you were naked, would you want someone to cover you? Can we honestly say we live this Scripture? Do we walk alongside it as if it was our best friend, dedicating our life to the growth and nourishment of the relationship? I noticed two very important words in the Scripture above which are "in everything." The Bible did not say treat people the way you want to treat them according to your mood. No, the Bible says, "So in everything, do to others what you would have them do to you, for this sums up the Law and the Prophets" (Matthew 7:12 NIV).

Now to answer our last question, **"How do we seek God's righteousness?"** Matthew 6:33(NIV), "But seek first his kingdom and his righteousness, and all these things will be given to you as well." **Righteousness** means acting in a morally correct manner, even when you're all alone, or should I say, especially when you're all alone. When you're in your car behind a slow driver, do you yell at the driver, marinating in your own frustration because you are the only one who really knows how to drive? Or, what happens to your moral behavior when you are in the express line with thirty items when the sign clearly states twelve items or less, LESS being the key word. Could this be considered moral behavior? What about after you finish putting your groceries in the car, what do you do with your cart? Not when the sun is shining and you just ran into some folks from church who may be watching. No, what do you do with your cart when it's freezing rain, and the wind is blowing 40 miles per hour and you're in a hurry, hungry, and cold. What do you do then with your cart?

Moral behavior is in everything you do and everywhere you go. It should follow you like a lost puppy who has found his owner. Remember the Scripture says in Matthew 6:33, "But seek first his kingdom and His righteousness, and all these things will be added to you." It is God's righteousness, His standard of moral behavior, not ours. Seldom do we think about our subtle attitudes as moral behavior, as doing to others as we would like to have done to us. But I believe our attitudes are just as important because our attitudes eventually form our words and our words eventually form our actions. As we are tapping our toes impatiently waiting for the world to recognize our need, we have fallen into a dangerous trap of becoming self-absorbed. The trap that was designed with one person in mind, "self." We have gone to extremes to find the word "one" in righteousness when we should have been more concerned with the word "the One." If you are never required to think about anyone but you, then you have allowed yourself to be number one in your life instead of "the One." When you are number one in your own life, what number is God?

Let's test ourselves with a few simple questions so we can have an intelligent, informed decision before we answer the question.

Choices are for the Living:

1. Who is your life about? Is it about God or about you?

_____
_____
_____
_____
_____
_____
_____
_____
_____
_____
_____
_____
_____

2. Consider the Scripture Matthew 7:12, "So in everything, do to others what you would have them do to you, for this sums up the Law and the Prophets." Do you live your life as if you believe this Scripture?

_____
_____
_____
_____
_____
_____
_____
_____
_____
_____
_____
_____
_____

3. When was the last time you did something for someone else that you would want done to you? What did you do and how did they respond? Wouldn't it be insane if we had a husband and wife fighting over who is going to get to give the other one a back rub or a foot massage? Or what about siblings fighting over who will be first to share whatever they have with the other one.

    _____
    _____
    _____
    _____
    _____
    _____
    _____
    _____
    _____
    _____
    _____
    _____

4. Are you a selfish person, meaning do you think about yourself more than others? When was the last time you did something for someone else when no one else was aware of it? How did they respond?

    _____
    _____
    _____
    _____
    _____
    _____
    _____
    _____
    _____
    _____
    _____
    _____

5. What pain from your past can you use for God's Glory?
    Write some ways you can use your past pain for God's
    Glory.

_____
_____
_____
_____
_____
_____
_____
_____
_____
_____
_____
_____

Weekly Challenge: Have your family go through their clothes,
then take your belongings to the homeless shelter. If you are a
beautician, volunteer to cut the hair of the people who live at the
shelter. Write about your experience.

Additional Notes:

_____
_____
_____
_____
_____
_____
_____
_____
_____
_____
_____
_____

Chapter 8

Just Because You Say "Lord, Lord," Doesn't Mean Your Name Is Written

*Matthew 7:21, "Not everyone who says to me, 'Lord, Lord,' will enter into the kingdom of Heaven, but only he who does the **will** of my Father who is in Heaven."*

Hebrews 10:5-7, "Therefore, when Christ came into the world, he said: "Sacrifice and offering you did not desire, but a body you prepared for me; with burnt offerings and sin offerings you were not pleased. Then I said, 'Here I am— it is written about me in the scroll-- I have come to do your will, O God.'"

*H*ave you ever thought that Jesus dying on the cross was the will of the Father? The awful way Jesus was crucified was His Father's will. Sometimes we like to paint a picture of God's will as a Van Gogh, a modern view of the present times, instead of a Picasso, a bit of an abstract view. Would God allow a moment of your peace to be obscured in order for a lifetime of peace to be instilled? I don't think God hides our peace, but I do believe He allows our choices to evacuate our peace.

"Going a little farther, he fell on his face to the ground and prayed, 'My Father, if it is possible, may this cup be taken from me. Yet not as I will, but as you will'" (Matthew 26:39). In Luke 22:44, "And being in anguish, he prayed more earnestly, and his sweat was like drops of blood falling to the ground." Jesus was in the garden in anguish, sweating drops of blood, praying that His Father would allow His cup, (His Father's will) to pass Him by, but "not as I will, but as you will." This does not resemble the peace you and I have been told about, but none the less, it is peace. Sometimes we think of peace as the absence of trouble, but in reality, peace is being able to walk out the will of God in the midst of your troubles. Peace allows you to be able to withstand the crucifixion, the crux of your infliction.

Maybe we think God's will is that we never experience trouble in this life, but God's Word clearly states we are to expect trouble, plan on it, because it will come according to John 16:33, " I told you these things, so that in me you may have peace. In this world you will have trouble. But take heart! I have overcome the world."

Here is a list of eyewitness martyrs as compiled from numerous sources outside the Bible, the most famous of which is Foxes' Christian Martyrs of the World:[24]

Stephen was preaching the gospel in Jerusalem on the Passover after Christ's crucifixion. He was cast out of the city and stoned to death. About 2,000 Christians suffered martyrdom during this time (about 34 A.D.).

James, the son of Zebedee and the elder brother of John, was killed when Herod Agrippa arrived as governor of Judea. Many early disciples were martyred under Agrippa's rule, including Timon and Parmenas (about 44 A.D.).

Philip, a disciple from Bethsaida, in Galilee, suffered martyrdom at Heliopolis, in Phrygia. He was scourged, thrown into prison, and afterwards crucified (about 54 A.D.).

Matthew, the tax-collector from Nazareth who wrote a gospel in Hebrew, was preaching in Ethiopia when he suffered martyrdom by the sword (about 60 A.D.).

James, the Brother of Jesus, administered the early church in Jerusalem and was the author of a book in the Bible. At the age of 94, he was beat and stoned, and finally had his brains bashed out with a fuller's club.

Matthias was the apostle who filled the vacant place of Judas. He was stoned at Jerusalem and then beheaded.

Andrew, the brother of Peter, preached the gospel throughout Asia. On his arrival at Edessa, he was arrested and crucified on a cross, two ends of which were fixed transversely in the ground (thus the term, St. Andrew's Cross).

Mark was converted to Christianity by Peter, and then transcribed Peter's account of Jesus in his Gospel. Mark was dragged to pieces by the people of Alexandria in front of Serapis, their pagan idol.

Peter was condemned to death and crucified at Rome. Jerome holds that Peter was crucified upside down, at his own request, because he said he was unworthy to be crucified in the same manner as his Lord.

Paul suffered in the first persecution under Nero. Because of the converting impact he was having on people in the face of martyrdom, he was led to a private place outside the city where he gave his neck to the sword.

Jude, the brother of James, was commonly called Thaddeus. He was crucified at Edessa in about 72 A.D.

Bartholomew translated the Gospel of Matthew in India. He was cruelly beaten and crucified by idolaters there.

Thomas, called Didymus, preached in Parthia and India. He was thrust through with a spear by pagan priests.

Luke was the author of the Gospel under his name. He traveled with Paul through various countries and was supposedly hanged on an olive tree by idolatrous priests in Greece.

Barnabas, of Cyprus, was killed without many known facts about 73 A.D.

Simon, surnamed Zelotes, preached in Africa and Britain, where he was crucified in about 74 A.D.

John, the "beloved disciple," was the brother of James. Although he suffered great persecution, including imprisonment where he wrote the book of Revelation, he was the only apostle who escaped a violent death.

Six times in the New Testament it says, "Paul an apostle of Jesus Christ by the will of God."[25] It was God's will that Paul was an apostle, but Paul was beheaded in Rome for the very thing God had willed him to do. We like to fantasize about the will of God in a field of daffodils beside a stream flowing with crystal clear water. We pray for God's will as flippantly as we pray for one another at times. How many times have you said and I said, "I will pray for you;" then our words fall silent upon the ground of good intentions, walked upon with guilt and shame when the person says later, "Thank you so much for praying for me." How authentically do we want the will of God in our everyday lives? Is the peace of God there while you are in His will even if His will doesn't look like peace? We must consider the Martyrs, were they in the will of God? If so, did their death resemble the peace you're familiar with? Could it be that the peace we have been taught about may be incomplete, not null and void altogether, just incomplete?

I believe we can have the kind of peace the Martyrs experienced. I believe in the midst of death, there can be life. How many times have you prayed Philippians 4:7, "And the peace of God, which transcends all understanding, will guard your hearts and minds in Christ Jesus." What do we think this passage is talking about? Peace is not positive thinking. You can't talk yourself into peace. You can't tap your heels three times, like Dorothy, and you're back in the house peace built, where Toto is wagging his tail, the tin man's heart is thumping at the perfect rhythm with the radio, the scarecrow develops a brain, the lion has courage and the wicked witch is dead. No! Peace is a condition of the mind, whatever goes into our minds, predestines our words. A martyr's death certainly transcends all of our understanding.

> Philippians 4:8, "Finally, brothers, whatever is true, whatever is noble, whatever is right, whatever is pure, whatever is lovely, whatever is admirable—if anything is excellent or praiseworthy---think about such things."

Peace comes from putting everything we know on the foundation of the Word of God. Peace knows God is in control, our destination has already been programmed, we're already pre- registered, our flight has been pre-paid. And when the sun darkens, the moon no longer gives us light, the stars have fallen from the sky and the heavenly bodies start to shake, then we will be the ones who are called to pre-board our flight with a one way ticket to Heaven.

As Solomon stated in Ecclesiastes 3:1-8, "There is a time for everything, and a season for every activity under heaven: a time to be born and a time to die, a time to plant and a time to uproot, a time to kill and a time to heal, a time to tear down and a time to build, a time to weep and a time to laugh, a time to mourn and a time to dance, a time to scatter stones and a time to gather them, a time to embrace and a time to refrain, a time to search, and a time to give up, a time to keep and a time to give away, a time to tear and a time to mend, a time to be silent and a time to speak, a time to love and a time to hate, a time for war and a time for peace."

How does this passage speak to you? It tells me there is a time for everything. There has been a plethora of people looking for a job lately. I think many of you would agree with me that it's God's will that you have a job, but you might go several months without one. Why? Because what God can teach you in the months to come could be more valuable than what you would have learned by getting a job straight away. It's all about the timing of God, but it's ironic because the hands on God's clock are His hands, which are not subject to our earthly time. The will of God can look different than the script you have played in your mind. Were the disciples in the will of God? Yes! Yet they experienced persecution. God's will for your life might not be the painted postcard you envisioned with waterfalls that cascade down a mountain carved into the life you dreamed of, but He will always supply His peace.

What if you knew exactly what the will of God was for your life. What if He showed you what His will was, but your life didn't end up well in the natural. The beginning of your life was good. You had God-fearing parents, your siblings and you got along for the most part; you had the story book childhood. Then you went off to college where you met your soul mate, you courted for several years then got married and had three beautiful children who obeyed you out of pure love, never rebelled and a dog named Rover who never pottied in the house and waited by the front door with your slippers. You were successful in your career of choice and you volunteered where your passion resided. Then one day, you heard God as you had never heard Him before, asking you to move your family overseas to become a missionary. You answered the call on your life and moved your family overseas. Then suddenly, out of nowhere, you were killed while doing what God had called you to do.

Would you still want His will in your life if you knew what the outcome would be? Do we love Him enough to lay down our lives for Him? Do I? I want to love my God that much. I want to be sold out that much. You need to stop right here, put down this book and ask yourself this question, "Do I really want the will of God in my life at all costs, or do I only want the postcard version of my life?" I really believe we would pray differently for God's will if we did not have a preconceived idea of what His will was. I have known people who have said these words to me, "If God calls me to go, He will not allow anything to happen to me." My response is simple, "Then how do you explain the Martyrs?" How do you read their stories and come up with that conclusion? Have we not received comfort in a poignant kind of way in their deaths that they died for Christ sake, and maybe, just maybe, we would do the same? Have we not recalled the cross more times than we can count? Why? Because in Jesus' death, there is hope, because it was the will of the Father that He be crucified on the cross so many would be saved.

What if your life was going to speak louder in your death than in your living, would you be willing to let your death have a voice? We are all going to die in the natural if the rapture does not come in our lifetime, but would you be so anxious to pray for God's will if you knew His will was for you to die a martyr's death? All of our lives eventually lead to our death, but the question is do we want God's will at all costs in our living and in our dying? I think with all fairness, for many of you, my question unfortunately would depend on what stage of life you're in. If you're just starting out in life, you might have a harder time wanting God's will at all costs. But if you're in your fifties or sixties, you might be willing to be sold out for the will of God.

I wonder how many people God has called to be missionaries, to minister overseas, to go into the prisons, to go to Africa, China, or India to help build churches, dig a well, feed the hungry, give medical attention to the dying, but because fear has captivated us, fear of the unknown, but not of the fear of God, we have chosen to be hunkered down in our own little subdivisions; that's called "Lord, Lord." This subdivision is beautiful; the flowers are in full bloom. Each house is well groomed with seasonal plants, water fountains and yard art. The birds are chirping, and there is a slight breeze coming in from the south while the children swim in the pools. The neighbors are exceptional, friendly, helpful, and even considered family, but is there more? Does God want us to do more than live in the confines of our own world? I believe He does. I believe God wants us to get in our cars and drive out of our neighborhoods into a world that is not our comfort zone, a world that needs a doctor because Jesus came for the sick. In Luke 5:31, "Jesus answered them, "It is not the healthy who need a doctor, but the sick. I have not come to call the righteous, but sinners to repentance." We are to do greater works than what Jesus did according to John 14:12.

> "Not everyone who says, "Lord, Lord," will enter into the kingdom of Heaven, but only he who does the will of my Father who is in Heaven" (Matthew 7:21).

Do you want God's will at any cost? My friend Kaye did. I would like to share her story in some of her own words. Read as Kaye opens her life and raw emotions as she experiences her faith journey on Mercy Ships.

Michele Davenport

I knew my profession as a nurse was my calling, for as long as I can remember I knew that's what I was supposed to do. I tried several areas of nursing from ER, maternity, women's health, and then finally ended up doing surgical nursing, mostly pre-op and post-op. Which now, I can clearly see what God could see all along. The surgical experience helped prepare me for Mercy Ships. In all my years of working in hospitals and for private surgeons, I knew it wasn't where my journey would end. God was (ALWAYS) tugging at my heart saying "this is not what I want you to be doing for a lifetime only for a moment." When I would ask Him what He wanted me to do, He never did say a word that I was able to hear in the natural, although I knew He had already spoken it into existence in the spiritual realm. So after several years of asking and hearing nothing, I finally decided to quit my job and trust God for the spiritual calling I always knew He had on my life. It was then that God began to open doors. While playing on Facebook one evening, I saw an ad for Mercy Ships. When I showed it to my husband, Tony, he immediately said that he believed that was what I needed to do, my first confirmation. The following Sunday, Pastor Mike Hernandez was speaking at Church of the Harvest and gave his testimony about quitting his job and waiting on the Lord for His direction, another confirmation. Lastly, I had a third confirmation through a sermon by Pastor Dave Beal. By this time I was fully convinced God had broken what appeared to be silence in my ear. It was as if God had tapped me on the shoulder with the words of other voices ringing in my ear.

So I began my application process to Mercy Ships. I never realized how many jobs were available on the ship, but the opportunities are abundant. So with everything in order, my husband and I decided if I was going to commit my talents to the Lord, we should make it worth the price of the plane ticket and stay longer than a week or two. In addition to our thoughts, the Ward Nurse positions required a minimum of eight weeks of commitment. Another option would have been to work the recovery room and stay anywhere from two weeks on, but the timing was not of God. The Ward Nurse position seemed to be the direction the Lord was taking me. I thought to myself eight weeks, no problem.

My adventure begins, two weeks pass and yes, I miss my family, especially Tony, but it's not as bad as I thought it might be. Three weeks pass then four weeks and I begin to wonder, "What was I thinking!" I don't think I can do this, Lord. It's too long to be away from my husband and family and of course, my husband, Tony is having a hard time as well. Not to mention, I struggle with vertigo. I didn't do well on the cruise I went on just a couple of months before coming to spend eight weeks on a ship. I assumed since the ship was in the port, docked the entire time, the motion would not be a problem. I was wrong! Even though the boat is docked it still moves with the heartbeat of the ocean. I honestly thought I needed to prepare myself for the idea of being nauseated for the remainder of my time I'm here. But God is SO gracious; He healed me of the vertigo. Yes, I still feel the heart of the ocean, but it is now beating with mine. Although, one night was exceptionally rough while lying in bed, struggling with the living pulse of the ocean, while missing my husband terribly, amidst my tears and inability to sleep, I reached for my Bible and it opened to Isaiah 43. It says this: "But now, God's Message, the God who made you in the first place, the One who got you started, don't be afraid, I've redeemed you. I've called your name. You're mine. When you're in over your head, I'll be there with you. When you're in ROUGH WATERS, you will not go down. When you're between a rock and a hard place, it won't be a dead end-- Because I am GOD, your personal GOD, The Holy of Israel, and your Savior. I paid a huge price for you...that's how much I love you! I'd sell off the whole world to get you back, trade the creation just for you."

God's written Word ministered to me while I laid there swaying to the movement of the call of God on my life. I've had peace surpassing all understanding since the Isaiah moment when God and I worked it out in the quietness of the moment. Granted I am still anxious, excited, and even overwhelmed at times to get home to see my husband, family and friends. I know I will make it through whatever my God has in store for me because my GOD who loves me so much, brought me here to do this work for HIS people who He also loves just as much. I am honored to be able to do the work for His kingdom. It has truly been the most fulfilling experience I have ever been a part of. Now that I have resonated myself with God's Word, I will not only survive my journey, but I will have peace during those moments of uncertainty. Then maybe someday, He'll call me and ask me to do it all over again, and my mind will quickly recall the night my heartbeat became one with Jesus in Isaiah 43. As I pack my bags I'll remember how He loves me and how He also loves the world. Miss Kaye

As I am writing this book, Kaye is on her second journey with Mercy Ships.

You might be thinking, that was a nice story but what I haven't told you was Kaye had to sign a legal document stating that if she was killed while serving on the Mercy ships, they had permission to ship her body back home. Kaye was willing to die to do the will of God in her life. Are you?

Choices are for the Living:

1. What if your life was going to speak louder in your death than in your living, would you be willing to let your death have a voice?

_____
_____
_____
_____
_____
_____
_____
_____
_____
_____
_____
_____

2. Have you ever thought that Jesus dying on the cross was the will of the Father? The awful way Jesus was crucified was the will of the Father. Sometimes we like to paint a picture of God's will as a Van Gogh, a modern view of the present times, instead of a Picasso, a bit of an abstract view. Would God allow a moment of your peace to be obscured in order for a lifetime of peace to be instilled and why do you carry this opinion?

_____
_____
_____
_____
_____
_____
_____
_____
_____
_____
_____
_____

3. How authentically do we want the will of God in our everyday lives? What has God called you to do? Are you pursuing God's will?

_____
_____
_____
_____
_____
_____
_____
_____
_____
_____
_____
_____
_____

4. "Do I really want the will of God in my life at all costs, or do I want the post card version? I really believe we would pray differently for God's will if we didn't have a pre-conceived idea of what His will is. How are you praying right now for God's will in your life?

_____
_____
_____
_____
_____
_____
_____
_____
_____
_____
_____
_____
_____

5. If God told you to sell everything and move to Africa, would you do it if you knew it was God? Are you willing to follow the Holy Spirit without knowing where He is leading you?

_____
_____
_____
_____
_____
_____
_____
_____
_____
_____
_____
_____
_____

Weekly Challenge: If you have never heard about World Vision, please go to their web-page www.worldvisiongifts.org. Ask God what He would like you to do for this organization, be open to hear and obey. They send free catalogs for you to look through. Pray for God's direction in the area you are felt led to be an answer to someone else's prayer.

Additional Notes:

_____
_____
_____
_____
_____
_____
_____
_____
_____
_____

Chapter 9

Worship In Spirit And In Truth

John 4:24, "God is spirit, and his worshippers must worship in spirit and in truth."

*Y*ou have the right to choose to praise God through your difficult times even if your difficult time is being thrown into an Indian prison like Pastor David encountered. Walk with me as Pastor David expresses his experience of how he learned to become a true worshipper in spirit and in truth.

In late March of 1995, I along with a team of pastors and lay leaders left a highly successful citywide healing evangelistic campaign in Rajahmundry, Andhra Pradesh, India for Bodapoda, Orissa, India. Rajahmundry's crusade had in excess of 40,000 in attendance each evening with over 1000 pastors receiving training each day. The 4 night crusade saw 45,000 come to Christ and was accompanied by healings and miracles of every kind.

Bodapoda was a very small village of approximately 1000 residents where the only building that was not a mud hut was a simple Baptist church that could seat maybe 150 by American standards. It was also a village in the middle of an Indian state that was entirely closed to the gospel and where the gospel and those who brought it were often persecuted and even killed for the sake of Christ.

A logistics team had gone before us, set up a gospel tent and promoted throughout the region that American preachers would come and share good news and heal the sick. The news spread like wildfire, and by the time we had arrived, the village had swelled from 1000 to an estimated 20,000 people.

Among the 20,000, there was also a contingency of 150 police that had confiscated the tent and would not allow us to leave the bus that we had arrived in. As some of our team negotiated with the police concerning allowing us to continue with the crusade, the rest of the police spent the better part of the afternoon trying to disperse the crowd by hitting them with 4 ft. bamboo sticks. By the end of that extremely long day, the police had managed to disperse approximately half of the crowd. It was painful to watch sincere, desperate people treated with such contempt and disregard.

The result of the day's negotiation was that we could only provide training to other Christians, that the tent would not be used and that we could do "Christian training" only in the Baptist church. As a part of the negotiation, we were told that there would be no tolerance for "proselyting" or "healing prayers." Because it had been an 11+ hour trip to the remote area, we agreed and began our "Christian training" event the next day.

The next day, we were met by thousands crowded in and around the small simple church building. Hundreds crammed into the building and thousands hovered outside the windows and doors to see and hear what was being taught and shared.

As the designated "healing evangelist" of our group, my role had changed to support and encouragement of the rest of our team as they shared on worship, pastoral ministry, outreach etc. As we moved to the lunch time, we cleared the small church and began feeding the crowd with curry and rice on banana leaves. It was then that a simple request and my response to it changed my life.

One of our team, Dr. Findlay Baird, had called for me to come outside to the front entry area of the church where he was standing with a small group of Indians that were interacting with him. When I arrived, he asked in his thick southern drawl if I would pray for a young boy that was standing in front of him with his father. The boy was born blind and he and his father had walked over 50 kilometers to receive healing. I immediately agreed, not thinking of the threats by the police the previous day, and upon praying, the young boy instantly received his sight!

Immediately following his healing, he began to joyfully yell out that he was healed, to which the small group of people outside the front door of that little church swelled to a crushing mass of humanity.

For approximately 10 to 15 minutes, Dr. Baird and I prayed for many people, all of who were gloriously healed! Having seen many healings and miracles over my many years of ministering for the Lord, I can truly say that I had never seen a greater, more sovereign move of God in healings and miracles than I saw in those few minutes. Every person prayed for was healed! No matter the condition! The blind saw, deaf heard, mute spoke, the lame walked, cancers and growths disappeared!

It was then that I noticed the helmets of the police as they began to form outside the mass of excited people. I suggested for the benefit of the people that we disengage and go inside before anyone was hurt or arrested. We pressed through the surging crowd to get inside the church building, and as we opened the doors to enter, it was like a broken levy that released a flood of people into the room.

The desperate people were clamoring for God's healing touch, so desperate that mothers were throwing their infant children over the crowd towards the platform for healing.

The police had seen enough and had begun trying to disperse the crowd by smashing those 4 foot bamboo sticks over the backs, shoulders and necks of those in the crowd. No matter how much we implored the crowd to calm down, they would not hear us. They wanted more of what God so freely gives. It was then that as a group we decided that leaving the area would help control the situation and minimize the dispersement efforts of the police on the people.

Upon leaving the church building, the police took us into custody and brought us down to the confiscated tent. I truly believe that at this time, the police were preparing to put us in our van with strict orders not to return, when the still excited people began gathering around the tent where we were being held. As Indian pastors and others would approach the police to intercede on our behalf, the police would beat and arrest anyone who dared approach. It was then that the police decided to disperse the crowd by using the former day's bullying tactics of beating the crowd with their sticks.

To this the people revolted and began throwing rocks at the police. The police ran for cover under their vehicles, being greatly outnumbered. The team and I immediately decided to intercede on behalf of the overwhelmed police by standing between them and the crowd. The crowd, honoring our efforts, stopped their attack almost immediately.

The police seeking to reinforce their authority, climbed out from under the vehicles they were hiding under and exchanged their 4 foot bamboo sticks for guns with which they immediately began firing into the crowds.

The miracle of moment was that having thousands standing tightly in the street, only one person was actually struck by a bullet and that in the leg.

At this point, we were loaded into a military troop truck and taken from the area. For two days and nights we drove not knowing where we were going or what our plight would be. Food and water was withheld and at times mental head games were employed to tease and torment us.

Finally, on the evening of the second day, we entered a small village and offloaded into a small mud house. Upon entering, it was clear that this was a court room and a judge was sitting behind a desk. Conversations were shared between those in charge and we were reloaded onto the truck and driven out of the village. After inquiring of one guard that had limited ability to speak English (and none of us spoke the language of the area), we discovered that we had been formally charged with crimes and were being sent to a high security prison in Berhampur, Orissa India. We were charged for attempted murder, resisting arrest, explosion of bombs and many other false charges.

This news was devastating having discovered that these were non-bailable charges and would have no chance of release while awaiting trial.

We arrived at the high security prison early afternoon the following day. After processing, we were released into the general prison population which we discovered later was 95% convicted murderers. We huddled together for about an hour in the middle of the prison yard. The commandant of the prison finally entered the yard and took us aside to a cleared area in the prison where we would spend the rest of our time.

The cell was approximately 20' X 20' and would house our entire team of 10 men. The cell was a single standing building with barred windows and a barred door. It was fully exposed to the elements, with a hard dirt/cement floor and green mold fully covering the walls; in the corner was a simple hole in the floor for a toilet and a single faucet of running water. This would be our home, our sanctuary and God's potter's wheel.

Why were we here? What was going on? When would it end? Did I do something wrong? Could I have done something to have avoided or changed the outcome of this situation? What about my wife Tracy, my daughters, church? Not being able to sleep or eat, I had plenty of time to think about these questions.

My answers were difficult to come by, but one thing was becoming clear, I was here because of a choice, a choice to pray for a young boy in need. That simple choice resulted in the experience that I was currently living through. And the choices I would make while in this place would determine everything.

It was during my prayerful consideration of these questions

Michele Davenport

that I asked God the simple understandable question, "Lord, when will I get out of here?" Then I heard the distinct voice of the Lord in my heart say, "When I'm done with you."

That answer told me several things. First was that my submission to the work of God in my life during this time was critical to my release. Second, that it was the Lord who was in control of this situation and not the Indian government, lawyers, the American consulate, media or money. Finally, these other men as well as my family would be affected by my cooperation with the Lord's work in this prison cell.

It was a regular practice of the group to gather in the middle of the cell for worship and prayer. It was during these times that we would share what the Lord was saying to us and to sing in praise and adoration to our Lord.

It was during these times that I discovered that my motivation was to manipulate God through my offerings of praise and worship to deliver us from our prison just like He did for Paul & Silas in Acts 16:25-26. I also discovered that our worship as a whole was not to the glory and honor of God but instead had what I call a "high whiny sound." The quality of the worship was more begging and mourning than true praise and worship. While it is natural to want to be delivered from difficult and adverse situations, God is jealous over worship. He desires that it be offered in Spirit and in Truth.

This discovery was enhanced by a visit from 2 high level Indian government officials, one a member of the high court and the other a member of the Prime Minister's second in command. Their visit was received with joy at first. After 6 days in an Indian jail cell with no food except some tangerines and some bottled water (both of which I was truly thankful), it was a sign of soon to come deliverance. It turned out that the opposite was true. Instead of news of our soon release, we were instead told that because of their laws and processes we could plan on staying in jail for at least 6 months, and that in a worst case scenario, we could be there for 10 years!

The officials encouraged us that they were working hard on our release and that they would be in touch through the commandant of the prison. With that, we thanked them for their efforts and said our goodbyes.

This news staggered us to the core. We all quietly went to our little areas of the cell and processed the information individually in our own ways. For me, the questions of how long, and what do I do now became my prayers to God. To my surprise, I had an immediate response from heaven. God clearly and distinctly spoke to my soul this message, "Stop crying and start praising Me."

"Lord, I have been praising You every day! And several times a day!" To that God simply reaffirmed the word, "Stop crying and start praising Me." This confronted my motivation, attitude and manner in praise and worship up to this moment.

To honor God's word to me, I spent the next couple of hours reaching a point of peace and release so that I could authentically praise and worship God without ulterior motives or intentions, and give Him the praise He deserved because of who He is, and not defining Him by my circumstances.

It was then time for us to gather as a group again (as was our custom) and process what we had heard and to share what we felt God was saying to each of us. It was then that I shared what I felt God had spoken, and a man in the group had had a similar word. In response, for the first time since our incarceration, we worshiped in Spirit and truth, singing and rejoicing in our Lord.

Now our group, while enthusiastic, was not going to give a concert or lead a worship service any time soon. We were flat, sharp, octaves out of range and off key. But we were real! In our worship, we reached the song "Glorify Your Name," a popular worship chorus of the late 70's early 80's. It was during this moment that I had, what I would call, a spiritual epiphany.

Suddenly the heavens opened and we were translated into the very throne room of God Himself. I heard the hosts of heaven singing with us! We were a part of the worship that is ever before the Throne! I understood something about true worship I had never fully understood.

First, that worship in spirit is eternal! It never dies or fades, even though we move on and do other things it remains a part of the eternal worship that is before the throne of God always. It joins the praise and worship of all who have ever worshipped in spirit and truth (John 4:24). It joins with Abraham, Isaac and Jacob's praise, with Moses, David, Daniel and the apostles, as well as all of the saints known and unknown!

Secondly, just as Paul saw and heard things that he was unable to share (2 Corinthians 12:1-4), I can say that there are notes, harmonies, melodies, octaves, and sounds that we have never heard that are in perfect harmony one with the other! It's AMAZING! Your eye has not seen nor has your ear heard (1 Corinthians 2:9)!

Finally, true worship with only the Glory and Honor of God and without ulterior motive or selfish ambition releases the presence and power of God into everything that is related to the one that is worshipping. This environment is the 'anything is possible' environment. This was evidenced by the return of the commandant of the prison within moments of the conclusion of our time of worship with the news that the prime minister of India had arranged for our release by paying $1,000,000 rupees a piece and ordering that we be taken to the airport by the police.

Within hours of the news of an extended stay in the prison by high level government officials, our circumstances had completely changed! God had moved supernaturally! On the seventh day of our imprisonment, we were released and began the long journey home, to the praise of His glory!

Choosing to follow the Lord is the greatest adventure of life. When we decide to give Him all and believe Him for what He says He will do, our lives will be consumed with life abundantly!

As I was reading in Hebrews 13:15, "Through Jesus, therefore, let us continually offer to God a sacrifice of praise - the fruit of our lips that confess His name," I never realized the Scripture said, "The fruit of our lips that confess His name." Readers, when we choose to praise God in our darkest situations, we are reaping the fruit of our lips in our outcome. As soon as Pastor David and his team started praising God from a place of authentic, genuine, worship, they were released from captivity. The fruit of their lips determined their outcome.

Praise turns our attention off of ourselves and onto God. We are acknowledging God's excellence. Many times, we mistake praising God as thanking Him, but praising Him is celebrating who God is, not what He has done or will do. Psalm 18:3, "I call to the Lord, who is worthy of praise, and I am saved from my enemies." Praising protects us in a way nothing else can. What was amazing to me was Pastor David, his team and the village people were shot at, but no one was killed, and only one hit, and in the leg at that. They were stuck in prison with murderers and no one was harmed; they were withheld food and water and no one took ill. Praise God, and in our praise, there is a protection that passes our understanding.

I couldn't help but think of all the inmates, the murderers, the thieves, the rapists and the molesters who were a witness to the Pastor and his team as they sang praises unto their Lord and Savior. 1 Peter 2:9, "But you are a chosen people, a royal priesthood, a holy nation, a people belonging to God, that you may declare the praises of him who called you out of darkness into his wonderful light." Wow!!! We are a witness to God's mercy and grace; we bring Him glory and allow others to see a glimpse of how wonderful our God is in every situation when we choose to praise Him in the storm. Proverbs 1:7, "The fear of the Lord is the beginning of knowledge, but fools despise wisdom and instruction." The New Testament believer wants to water down the Scriptures that say fear the Lord. They want to reduce the Scriptures to say, obey, love, reverence and worship, but that is not what it says fear is. You and I don't get to decide what word we are more comfortable using instead of the word fear. Just because we have decided to pin another name on fear does not mean it's a valid definition. Choices are for the living and the choices we make many times are made out of our emotions, other people's opinions and out of our life experiences, not necessarily out of the fear of the Lord. Many who might have been in the same predicament might have chosen to fear the official government, the possibility of residing in prison for 10 years, or the murderers who became their roommates, but Pastor David did not take the Word of the Lord lightly on that day in the court yard of the prison. I believe he feared the Lord and knew his choices would dictate his outcome.

> Psalm 112:1-10, "Praise the Lord. Blessed is the man who fears the Lord, who finds great delight in his commands. His children will be mighty in the land; the generation of the upright will be blessed. Wealth and riches are in his house, and his righteousness endures forever. Even in darkness light dawns for the upright, for the gracious and compassionate and righteous man. Good will come to him who is generous and lends freely, who conducts his affairs with justice. Surely he will never be shaken; a righteous man will be remembered forever. He will have no fear of bad news; his heart is steadfast, trusting in the Lord. His heart is se-

cure, he will have no fear; in the end he will look in triumph on his foes. He has scattered abroad his gifts to the poor, his righteousness endures forever; his horn will be lifted high in honor. The wicked man will see and be vexed, he will gnash his teeth and waste away; the longings of the wicked will come to nothing."

After reading the Scriptures, there are some clear character traits to someone who fears the Lord. Some of those are gracious, just, steadfast, cares for the poor and trusts the Lord. As well as character traits, there are benefits to fearing the Lord. Some of them are children who succeed, wealth and riches, light in the darkness, good follows him, great reputation, does not fear his enemies and he is honored. We need to welcome the fear of the Lord into our lives as we would a long lost friend. We need to hug it out with our God and allow Him to grow us up in this area of our walk with Him. I can hear some of you saying right now, "Fearing God is an Old Testament theory, we are New Testament believers with New Testament theories and we serve a God of love not fear." Let me grab a match to light the fuse that will blow your thinking out of the water. Acts 9:31, "Then the church throughout Judea, Galilee and Samaria enjoyed a time of peace. It was strengthened; and encouraged by the Holy Spirit, it grew in numbers, living in the fear of the Lord."

Wow!!! Did the New Testament Scriptures just say the church was strengthened, encouraged, and grew in numbers as they were living in the fear of the Lord? Where could their fear come from? Maybe it can be found in Acts 5:5-10 where Ananias and Sapphira dropped dead from lying. Maybe, just maybe, they took God at His Word. In Psalm 77:11 - 12, "I will remember the deeds of the Lord; yes, I will remember your miracles of long ago. I will meditate on all your works and consider all your mighty deeds."

For many of us, that Scripture means I will remember You raising the dead, allowing a blind man to see, opening the ears of a deaf man, turning water into wine, giving a voice to a donkey and parting the Red Sea, but having two people drop dead instantly for lying is a miracle as well. We would do ourselves a great justice if we would choose to remember the same God who cleansed the lepers, placed a coin in a fish's mouth, welcomed the thief on the cross into paradise and turned five loaves and two fish into a buffet to feed 5,000, as the same God who dropped Ananias and Sapphira to the ground. In Acts 5:11, the Word of God says, "Great fear seized the whole church and all who heard about these events." Oh readers, I pray for the day great fear seizes the New Testament church. We need to stop pretending we only serve a God who performs the miracles we enjoy.

Choices are for the Living:

1. How do you praise God?

_____

_____

_____

_____

_____

_____

_____

_____

_____

_____

_____

_____

2. When was the last time you worshipped God authentically during a difficult time? What were the results of that kind of praise?

_____

_____

_____

_____

_____

_____

_____

_____

_____

_____

_____

_____

3. Would you have prayed, like Pastor David, for the people in India knowing you might end up in prison and why? Be honest with yourself, it is okay not to know the answer. The purpose of the question is for you to examine your heart.

_____
_____
_____
_____
_____
_____
_____
_____
_____
_____
_____
_____
_____
_____

4. Write down when the last time your praise was a witness to someone else. What was their reaction to your choice to praise God instead of being angry?

_____
_____
_____
_____
_____
_____
_____
_____
_____
_____
_____
_____
_____
_____

5. Re- read Hebrews 11:15 and then define the term "sacrificial praise." According to the Scripture, how do we bring a sacrifice of praise?

_____
_____
_____
_____
_____
_____
_____
_____
_____
_____
_____
_____
_____
_____

Weekly Challenge: This week I want you to look for an opportunity to praise God in an authentic way. Praise Him no matter what happens this week because of who He is, even if you end up in an Indian prison; He is still God. Take time to recognize the world around you and praise God for His creativity.

Additional Notes:

_____
_____
_____
_____
_____
_____
_____
_____
_____
_____
_____
_____
_____
_____

Chapter 10

In The Future, When Your Children Ask You, Tell Them

Joshua 4:6, "In the future, when your children ask you, 'What do these stones mean?' tell them

Joshua 4:1-7, "When the whole nation had finished cross-ing the Jordan, the Lord said to Joshua, 'Choose twelve men from among the people, one from each tribe, and tell them to take up twelve stones from the middle of the Jordan from right where the priests stood and to carry them over with you and put them down at the place where you stay tonight.' So Joshua called together the twelve men he had appointed from the Israelites, one from each tribe, and said to them, 'Go over before the ark of the Lord your God into the middle of the Jordan. Each of you is to take up a stone on his shoulder, according to the number of tribes of the Israelites, to serve as a sign among you. In the future, when your children ask you, 'What do these stones mean?' Tell them that the flow of the Jordan was cut off before the ark of the covenant of the Lord. When it crossed the Jordan, the waters of the Jordan were cut off. These stones are to be a memorial to the people of Israel forever.'"

*I*n Deuteronomy 6:12, there is a beautiful warning, "Be careful not to forget the Lord, who brought you out of Egypt." It's interesting to me what the word "memorial" means in Hebrew. It means to remember. Stacking your stones is not to mark a place of burial or temple, but a memorial to some sort of battle. A memorial reminds us of a place or time in our lives; it triggers a memory good or bad. The Israelites were always forgetting about the Lord's goodness. I know many people who visit their past only to be tormented by the actions and reactions of others, but the Lord is saying, "Be careful not to forget your God who brought you out of Egypt." What has been your Egypt? Has the Lord brought you through a drug addiction? Has He brought you through being molested as a child or being raped? Or maybe God has brought you through a pornography habit, a cigarette habit or an ugly divorce. Or perhaps the Lord has brought you through cancer, an eating disorder, fear, stroke, suicidal thoughts or the loss of a loved one. Be careful readers, not to forget the Lord who brought you out of your Egypt.

When I look back on my own life, I have a choice to make. I can remember how God brought me through, or I can remember Egypt. I can remember slavery, or I can remember the sound of the handcuffs being unlocked as I felt my wrists being set free. I can remember the bondage I endure, or I can remember the aroma of my deliverance. Oh readers, how our memories remind us of God's faithfulness; it is a signpost planted firmly upon the ground to a lost world. The Apostle Paul says in Philippians 3:13 (NKJV), "I forget about the past so I can press on to the future." Isaiah said in Isaiah 43:2-3, "When you pass through the waters, I will be with you; and when you pass through the rivers, they will not sweep over you. When you walk through the fire, you will not be burned; and the flames will not set you ablaze. For I am the Lord, your God, the Holy one of Israel, your Savior; I give Egypt for your ransom, Cush and Saba in your stead." Wow! This tells me we are not only supposed to survive the waters, rivers, and fire, but God will lead us through without drowning in our disappointments or getting consumed by the fire of frustration.

Back to the stones, each stone represented a person, a tribe, if you will, and how God brought them through the Jordan to get to the other side. Many of you are still waiting on the wrong side of the Jordan. You are pining for Egypt because it's far easier to remain in the pain of your past than to pick up your stone and carry it across, but you must pick up your stone, hoist it upon your shoulders and carry it across. Then, lay it at the feet of Jesus. I believe the stone was a type and shadow of their previous bondage, despair and suffering. It represented God's ability to bring them through the trials of the promise of long ago according to Exodus 3:8, "So I have come down to rescue them from the hand of the Egyptians and to bring them out of that land into a good and spacious land, a land flowing with milk and honey." Another interesting tidbit, in Hebrew, "milk" represents spiritual, and "honey" represents the best. So in essence, the Lord was saying I have come down to deliver you from your oppression into a land filled with My spiritual best.

In Deuteronomy 1:6-7, "The Lord your God has said to us at Horeb, 'You have stayed long enough at this mountain. Break camp and advance into the hill country of the Amorites...'" Readers, for many of you God is saying, "You have stayed long enough at this mountain, break camp and advance; you have stood too long in front of a mountain that has been moved. I have offered you a land flowing with My spiritual best, pick up your stone and carry it across because one day your children will ask, 'What do these

Michele Davenport

stones mean?'" Each battle you've endured in your life is another opportunity to stack a victory stone as your signpost of faith. Your stones are your stories; they are the vehicle that is used to build your faith for your next story, your next testimony. We build our memorial by stacking our stones in remembrance to God.

I went to a nursing home to conduct church for the elderly. My message was on stacking your stones for Jesus. I asked them if they would be willing to be a part of a book I was going to write. I remember clearly, a lady name Barb, small in frame and gigantic in faith. As she sat there with one leg and a huge smile, she began to tell how she stacked her stones for Jesus. Barb recalls in 1990, she began having trouble with vascular disease. The pain had gotten so bad that the doctor had suggested that he take the veins out of the right leg and put them into the left leg. Barb agreed, but the veins did not take, so the only solution was to amputate Barb's left leg. After the amputation, Barb always had a great attitude about life and her God. She learned to depend on the Jordan--the embankment that could have held her hostage to her stone, the flowing of the waters that had the potential to wash over her had she not taken a step of faith, the obedience of picking up her stone, and the peace of knowing what was on the other side of her journey across the Jordan. Even the stacking of the stones became a part of her healing, because as she stacked one, she remembered how God brought her through the others. As Asaph cried out to God in his despair and doubt in the book of Psalm, this is what he found himself saying in 77:11-12, "I will remember the deeds of the Lord; yes, I will remember the miracles of long ago. I will meditate on all your works and consider all your mighty deeds." "Meditate" means "to reflect, spend time thinking and to plan." The word "consider" means "to think about in order to make up one's mind, to take into account, to believe." Barb did this in such a way that she found she'd lost her leg but not her God, she had lost her chance to run, but not her chance to walk with her Lord and Savior. She had lost her ability to let both feet hit the floor, but not the ability to let both hands hit the sky in awe of her God and His grace to see her through.

Barb sat quietly in front of me for a moment. As she gathered her thoughts, she began to tell me about her husband, Jerry. He held Bible studies at the Postal office where he worked. Jerry sowed seeds into his co-workers up to the day he met Jesus. She lost her husband October 11, 1973 at the age of 28. He was riding his motorcycle when a lady ran a red light. It was a hit and run. Barb was three months pregnant at the time of the accident. With prayer as her constant language, Barb survived yet another trip across the Jordan as she carried her stone and placed it at the feet of Jesus. She caught a glance at the stones before the one she was carrying. She noticed none were quite as heavy, none quite as hard to bear, none that brought her as much grief, but all of her grief had a significant role to play in building her faith muscles as she carried each stone across. It was all the stones before this one, on this day, that allowed her the faith to carry the tomb stone of her husband across to the other side.

During Barb's life, she has had numerous surgeries, died on the operating table twice and God brought her back. Barb has crossed the Jordan carrying her stones more times than not, but as she grew older, her faith muscles grew stronger and her stones became lighter, because we all eventually cast our cares upon Jesus.

I am reminded of a time recently that I had to take that walk across the Jordan carrying a stone I thought at the time was too heavy to bear. I will quote from my book "*Ripened on the Vine.*"

"Soon after we arrived in Missouri I realized how sick my mom was. It seemed as if she had aged on the inside about twenty years since I had seen her last. When I looked at her, I did not see her life flash before me, I saw mine. I saw the mom I had when I was a little girl. I saw the mom I had when I got married. I saw the mom I had when I got pregnant. I saw the mom I had when I gave birth, when I needed to talk, when I needed to cry, and when I needed a friend. My life had been reconciled, my mother had been restored to motherhood, the dreams of having a family had been realized and enjoyed. As I watched my mother deteriorate in front of my very eyes, the only memories I had were ones of appreciation. I appreciated my mom's willingness to fight. I appreciated her determination to live, if not for herself, then for me.

As I watched how every breath she took was an effort, I was convicted for wanting her to fight anymore. My mom had spent a lifetime fighting either a drug addiction, an alcohol addiction, a prescription drug addiction, a nicotine addiction or a self-loathing addiction. I could plainly see not only her body, but also her mind, was exhausted. Not only did my mom fight the addictions, but

Michele Davenport

she also fought a lifetime of manic depression. For the next seven months, my mom was in and out of hospitals, fighting to live while dying. I became a witness to her life as well as her death. Each day meant more than the last, each breath was honored as a will to fight, each smile was savored, and every laugh was captured in my mind. As I watched this woman that I called mom hold on to her fleeting life, I realized we did not have much time left on this earth together. Although I would not admit this in the midst of my surroundings, looking back, I know that I knew time was short.

There are few times in one's life that a memory becomes etched so deeply that it's like an artist has painted on the canvas of your heart with that particular point and time. If I were to hang the art on the wall of my mom's last hours, this is what you might have seen.

A grown women sitting in a chair next to her mother, singing her to sleep, a room full of people who love her, her grandchildren, her dedicated husband of twenty-one years, a loving sister and brother, her son-in-law, her pastor, and other friends and family. You might have even seen a Coke can with a straw hanging over the edge, because my mom loved Coke. You probably noticed the cup of ice chips to keep her lips moist, and the missing life support. You might have seen my mother in her blue hospital gown, and you may have noticed the empty coffee cups in fear of missing one moment of her life.

But as you stare at the painting, you probably didn't notice the grip the daughter had on her mother's hand, you might have missed her leaning over to whisper in her mother's ear, "It's okay, mom, if you want to let go now, I will be okay." You might have missed the look on the daughter's face after she said those words to her mother, the look of devastation, the look of fear, fear of losing one of her best friends, her look of emptiness and desperation. You might have missed the untold story of how this mother was her daughter's hero. You also might have missed the daughter silently bowing her head as if to say, "I trust you, Lord." But there is one thing I know you could not miss which is the love that filled the room where my mother laid, the peace that surpasses all understanding, the unity in letting go, the grace that abounds, and the hope in our living God.

Although a painting can speak volumes, the way one lives and dies speaks at a higher tone. As my mother was encompassed with the love of her family and her God, she took her last breath and went to meet Jesus on December 12ᵗʰ, 2006.

It's been over 5 years since my mother graduated to heaven, God has been faithful. To say we picked up the pieces and went on would be a lie, because my mother did not leave pieces behind. She left us whole, she left us strong in our faith, she left us peace in our hearts, and she left us knowing her God would hold us together. We have continued on in our faith and our journey here on earth. Marty and I are standing united in Faith Builders Ministries where we preach the good news of our Savior Christ Jesus. "

I pray by letting you see a glimpse of my life that it may witness God's mercy and grace in yours. My prayer for you also is that you will always walk in forgiveness, love from Heaven, and tell your story with a purpose. At the time of my mother's death, the water looked too deep to approach, the walk looked too long to endure, and the stone felt too heavy to carry, but as I stuck a toe in the Jordan, the waters receded, my feet were fitted with the gospel of peace, my stone no longer outweighed my faith. Before I realized my journey had started, I was on the other side. As I stacked my stone next to the many others in my life, I too remembered the miracles of long ago. Every other stone before now strengthened me for this one, and this stone will strengthen me for the next. These are called my "*faith builders.*"

Some of you are on the wrong side of the Jordan, and your stone has become too heavy to carry. You are too overcome by guilt and condemnation to ever enter into the promise land God has promised you. You have allowed Satan's lies to become your truth, your pain to become your prison. You must realize the only thing between the Israelites and their promised land was the Jordan; all they had to do was put a foot in the river and expect a miracle. The people who want to partake in God's spiritual best must allow the process of examining the pain of the past and then be willing to be washed by the watering of God's Word.

Here is a story about a lady who not only picked up her stone marked with the mark of date rape but allowed her God to escort her to the other side to her promise land filled with milk and honey, God's spiritual best. I believe God's spiritual best is to worship Him freely without the hindrances of our past, without the weight of condemnation and without the guilt of perfectionism before peace. God is a God of love wrapped in mercy, delivered with grace.

Hi, my name is Lori and one of the heaviest stones I've ever had to carry was hurled at me when I was 15 years old. It was more like a boulder than a stone, and when it hit, it crushed me into a million different pieces. It was late in the afternoon on St. Patrick's Day and the 16 year old boy I liked dropped by my house and asked if I could go for a drive. Surprisingly, my parents gave me permission and I willingly slid into his passenger seat. As he began to drive, I quickly realized he was getting further and further away from any place familiar, and eventually he pulled the car over in a secluded wooded area. What happened next became the weight of a thousand stones I would carry for years to come. I was date raped. For almost two hours, he violated me and nothing I could say would make him stop. When he was finally finished, he took me home and left as if nothing at ever even happened.

But something *had* happened...something devastating and I did not know where to turn. My parents and I struggled with communication and trust issues at the time, so I was afraid if I told them, they wouldn't believe me. Instead, I turned to one of my closest friends. The second blow came in her response. Once I shared my story with her, she simply replied, "You must have done something to ask for it." And this was my friend! The only one I trusted to believe me, and yet, she didn't. I was devastated again! News of what happened quickly spread around school, and I began to see that everyone else shared her opinion as well. Knowing what everyone thought of me and still having to sit in class with this boy every day was almost more than I could bear. Almost overnight, I had been given a reputation that I did not deserve. I was so broken inside and so humiliated, that over time, all of the hurtful words and lies spoken to and about me began to take their toll. Even I started believing the things being said...and their lies became my truth. I decided if that was who they thought I was, then that is who I would be.

At that point, my life really began to spiral out of control. Promiscuity and partying defined me. All of my self-worth was derived from empty, shallow relationships and yet, they always left me feeling even worse about myself. I was willing to do anything to be accepted and still always felt rejected. And the pain, shame and guilt never went away. These choices had other repercussions as well, including various female health problems and a lengthy struggle with infertility for years after I was married. It was during the first of these health scares that I began to cry out to God. I was raised in a Christian home and saved when I was six, and though I knew God, I was not submitted to Him. But at 21 years of age, God not only healed my body, He began picking up the pieces of my broken life. I rededicated my life to the Lord, married a wonderful man who also gave His heart to the Lord and finally set my feet on the path God had planned for me...but I was still in bondage.

I had long since left my deceived lifestyle behind, but the scars of guilt, shame and pain remained. And unfortunately, those scars continued to define my self-worth. No matter how many times I reminded myself, that I was a new creation and pure and holy in His sight, I just couldn't shake the condemnation of the enemy. Many more years passed and then God led me to my first small group Bible study. It was through this study that I began meditating on Isaiah 61:1-4 and God revealed to me my own bondage and captivity. He lovingly showed me how much He wanted to heal my broken heart, free me from my captivity and release me from my bondage. He wanted to comfort me, exchange my ashes for His beauty, my mourning for His joy, my heaviness for His praise. And He wanted to rebuild and restore those places within me that had long been devastated. Isaiah 61 became my Jordan River. And as I stepped into it...heart, mind and soul...He set me free! And through His faithfulness, unconditional love and endless mercy, my crushing boulder became a precious memorial stone to my incredible Savior. "Therefore if the Son makes you free, you shall be free indeed (John 8:36)."

I can relate to Lori's story because I too have been date/relationship raped. I chose to live with a guy whom I was in a relationship with. Because I had chosen to live with him, he thought he could rape me. It breaks my heart when a woman gets violated in this way, partly because of the violent act that has been hoisted against her body, but more so of the brokenness that is left behind way after the rape kit is put away and her body has been washed. Far beyond the police report, extended beyond the sympathetic looks, and the mockery of feeling like you deserved it or that everyone knows your secret. It is in this kind of brokenness that the pain haunts your every thought, your every move, and your every attempt to be normal again; to look at yourself in a mirror without judging your self-worth for their sin.

The first time my body had been violated in this manner was when I was eleven at an amusement park. The next time was with the guy I had chosen to live with and the last time was by my uncle in my teens. Where did I find my healing? In was in Jesus' presence, it was in His Word. It was in 2 Corinthians 5:17, "Therefore if anyone is in Christ, he is a new creation; the old has gone, the new has come!"

When I was twenty-two, I was reunited with Christ. I found my Deliverer, my Healer, and the Restorer of my life. I found that I was a new creation, the old was gone, meaning the old me, the old broken, abused, and neglected me was gone and new had come to release me from all the condemnation I had carried for all those years. I too, had to carry my rape stone across the Jordan, and as I was walking, my eyes caught a glimpse of my Jesus, the nails in His hands were still evident of the stone He also carried on my behalf. Oh readers, you may feel like you've had forty lashes minus one from this world; you may feel like you have been mocked, ridiculed, and set aside to die a horrible death, but Jesus showed us how to live in His dying. Jesus showed us how to roll the stone away in victory. He confessed with His mouth that the temple (referring to His body) would be destroyed but would rise again after three days.[26] It's in our confession that we are saved. It's with our confession we are set free. It's in our own obedience to the God we serve when we choose to place a foot in the Jordan. Then and only then will the river stand on its head and let us carry our memorial stone into the promise land, a land flowing with God's spiritual best, a land that has been holding its breath to receive us.
Indulge me as we read about another friend of mine and her journey across the Jordan.

My name is Debi and I was not raised in a Christian home. I met my boyfriend when we were teenagers but today we have been married for over 25 years. I hated men and I hated sex (because of past history of men) so I tried to steer completely from both. Thinking what in the world is wrong with me? One thing that drew me to my boyfriend was that he loved me for me at the level that he knew love. He did not want me for an object of his lust but saw something different in me that other guys did not see. I came from a dysfunctional home and love was just not displayed or felt in our home. Well, eight months into our relationship we were drinking; one thing led to another and I had sex for the very first time. Yes you guessed it, I became pregnant. You see, I was already dealing with so many wounds, hurts and pain from my past. Now on top of all those emotions, I find myself having to make one of the biggest decisions of my life. Would I have our baby or would I abort our baby? I did not give my boyfriend a choice on whether our baby would live or die. I just told him what we would do. My mother said I could keep the baby or abort the baby. The choice was mine but I saw no way out. How could I raise a child? We were drinking, doing drugs and had our priorities out of order. We didn't know how to prioritize our lives, so how could we bring a baby into the world when our world was so messed up. I wasn't emotionally stable enough to make this decision! Well, I chose the abortion. Oh, I wish I would have known Jesus. Oh, how I wish I would have known the Scriptures that are so embedded in my heart today. Jeremiah 1:5, *"Before I formed you in the womb I knew you, before you were born I set you apart; I appointed you as a prophet to the nations."* Psalm 139:13, *"For you (God) created my inmost being: you knit me together in my mother's womb."* God knew my baby before my baby would be born. I type this with tears running down my cheeks. God was creatively forming my baby's little body. How I wish I would have known then what I know now. God can take our mess and make it His mess; bringing wholeness to the situation if we would just trust Him.

My emotions were off the chart. The emotions of shame, torment, guilt, condemnation, blame, anger, sense of hopelessness at times, bitterness, un-forgiveness and grief. All the emotional pain of the abortion clinic, the people shouting outside and the drugs they give you. Year after year, I wonder about the sex of my baby, my baby's birthday, and who the baby would have looked like. I will say this was a little overwhelming for a teenager. I was so wounded and did not know how to reach out for my healing. Well, in 1992 I asked Jesus in my heart and became a born again Christian and the healing began. His Word says in 2 Corinthians 5:17, "Therefore if anyone is in Christ, he is a new creation; the old has gone, and the new has come." That if I had Jesus in my heart that He would be faithful to forgive me of my sins. I just needed to ask, believe and receive. He put so many tools in my hands to bring about His healing in me in this area of my life. Salvation, the Word of God (His Bible), older women in the faith coming alongside me, 'Celebrate Recovery' group, and a book called *Ripened on the Vine*. Sitting at His feet just seeking God, my friend and this book (*Ripened on the Vine*) were very crucial in bringing about the healing I so desperately needed in my life. Little by little, God started mending and stitching me. I had so much to be healed of there was no way the surgeon could have completed all the surgeries at once. No, it was a process. The Bible calls it "from glory to glory." We are transformed into His likeness and into His image, 2 Corinthians 3:18. The Great Physician is still doctoring me up today. See the devil comes to steal, kill and destroy but God has come to give us life abundantly. Satan is the father of Lies and God is our Father of Truth. Who is your daddy? Which one will you believe?

In the Message Bible, we read that we are an open book for others to read. I open my book of brokenness which turned into wholeness. My desire for you is to read the ink off of the pages of my heart so it will bring you the complete healing you may need through my testimony. I have battled this demon for 29 years. I share this as I take my stone across the Jordan River. When my friend, Michele, asked me to do this, I was definitely a little hesitant, but I knew God was in it and it was not about me but about God and allowing Him to receive all the Glory out of my brokenness. I know now as I carry my abortion stone to the other side, I will be completely whole in this very personal area of my life. I can say I actually feel the freedom with tears in my eyes as I type out my feelings upon this paper. My life is not my own; it has been bought with a price, the blood of Jesus. I am here to finish the work He has called me to do and to glorify my Master and Savior. I cannot change anything in my past, but I can change my today and my future. Out of my transparency and my brokenness, I can be a forerunner for Jesus, telling of His goodness, and what He did for me, He will do for you. I wrote this poem in honor of my unborn child.

You Were The One

You were the one I thought about all those years

Yes it was hard shedding fountains of tears

Oh how I longed to see your face

I only made it because of God's grace.

I am so sorry that you had to die

I did not know the truth, I bought into the lie

Year after year I thought how old would you be

No longer tormented, God is setting me free.

I did not mean for you to die such a terrible death

As you entered heaven, God gave you new breath

God is slowly erasing all of the pain

He has promised forgiveness and a cure for the stain.

I know you are in heaven, yes Jesus and you

I will be there someday, open the gate let me through

Thank Jesus for me for making a way

I love you so much and can't wait for that day.

If you have experienced the stone I am talking about please pray this prayer with me.

Dear Lord, Thank You that You love me with an everlasting love. According to Your Word, Your love will not fail me. You sent your only Son for me. Wow! Now that is really a lot of love. Oh, I want to live for You and live a life of freedom. Come into my heart, Jesus. I ask You to forgive me. You say in Your Word that You will forgive my sins as far as the east is from the west. You remember them no more, so neither should I remember sins You have blotted out. Oh Jesus, thank You for forgiving me, and by faith, I also forgive____ _____, _____, _____ (Add the people that you need to forgive). I now know that forgiveness is not a feeling; it is a gift to myself and a gift to those that I am choosing to forgive right now. Help me with all of these out-of-control emotions. Help me to have a sweet sleep tonight. Thank You for Your grace and that You are a God of second chances. Old things have passed away and behold all things become new in my life. I am a new creation and I have a new mind. When You set us free, we are free indeed. There is no more condemnation, guilt, shame, torment, sorrow, grief, pain, hurt or sadness. You are the Prince of Peace, Lord. Thank You for that peace that is now flooding my soul. I trust you, Lord. Thank You for comforting me and seeing me across the Jordan while I to carry my stone to place as a memorial to Your faithfulness. I now have a sound mind, Your mind, and a peace that will pass my understanding. No longer can the enemy torment me because the Lord came to destroy the works of the devil, to give me life more abundantly and to the fullest. When You set me free, I was free indeed. Amen[27].

We all have stones in our lives that will eventually need to be carried across the Jordan. The question is will you choose to cross over to the Promise Land or remain on the edge of the river?

Choices are for the Living:

1. What stones do you need to carry across the Jordan?

_____
_____
_____
_____
_____
_____
_____
_____
_____
_____
_____
_____

2. What lifestyle do you need to leave behind?

_____
_____
_____
_____
_____
_____
_____
_____
_____
_____
_____
_____

3. Is there a tomb stone that you have been sleeping with every night that you need to let go of? If so, who is it and why do you feel like you must hold onto their death?

_____
_____
_____
_____
_____
_____
_____
_____
_____
_____
_____
_____
_____

4. Is there a rape stone you need to carry across that's marked with forgiveness?

_____
_____
_____
_____
_____
_____
_____
_____
_____
_____
_____
_____
_____

5. Do you have an abortion stone to carry? Pray for forgiveness and then walk to other side where God's spiritual best is waiting for you.

_____
_____
_____
_____
_____
_____
_____
_____
_____
_____
_____
_____
_____
_____

Weekly Challenge:

I have several challenges for you to choose from this week.

- The first challenge is to volunteer at abortion clinic.

- The second challenge is if you have been raped (and 1 out of 3 women have been sexually assaulted, so that means 1 out of the 3 women who read this book have been violated in this way), share your story with someone you trust. Revelation 12:11, "*They overcame him by the blood of the Lamb and by the word of their testimony.*"

- The last challenge is if you have been date raped and have not forgiven the person who assaulted you in this way - repeat this prayer with me:

Lord, I choose to forgive _____ for violating me in this way. I choose to walk a walk of love, knowing it costs a price to be obedient to Your Word. I, by faith, forgive my abuser so I do not keep myself handcuffed to their sin but allow myself the freedom to forgive and move forward with my life. Lord, please allow me to walk in the light of what You have done for me, the forgiveness You have shown me, the grace You have instilled upon my life and the mercy that I receive new every morning. Amen.

Write about what challenge you chose to do.

Additional Notes:

_____
_____
_____
_____
_____
_____
_____
_____
_____
_____
_____
_____
_____
_____
_____
_____
_____
_____
_____
_____
_____
_____
_____

Chapter 11

All Of This Because We Refuse To Move Forward Yesterday

Numbers 14:3, "Wouldn't it be better for us to go back to Egypt"

*Numbers 14:1-3, "That night all the people of the commu-
nity raised their voices and wept aloud. All the Israelites
grumbled against Moses and Aaron, and the whole assem-
bly said to them, 'If only we died in Egypt! Or in the desert!
Why is it that the Lord is bringing us to this land only to let
us fall by the sword? Our wives and children will be taken as
plunder. Wouldn't it be better for us to go back to Egypt?'"
Egypt represented bondage.*

*I*t is here where the Israelites came to a crossroads, the sign in
the road which read belief or unbelief, bondage or freedom.
They were either going to enter into the promise land or stand on
the other side. It's a place of decision, a place to agree to meet God
at the crossroads of His Word. Amos 3:3, "Do two walk together
unless they have agreed to meet?" God and you must agree to meet
in order to walk together. In other words, if you want to be walking
in His footsteps for your life, you must agree to meet Him before
you take off walking.

The Israelites fell short when it came to this very thing. They
had a bad habit of walking without meeting with God. God would
speak, they would listen, and then they would make decisions based
out of their fear of people, situations and circumstances rather than
on their fear of the Lord. I began to ponder this, what if you and I
had the chance to see what they had seen? Could you imagine being
there in a time where your enemy was chasing you to the frazzled
hem of the deep Red Sea? You are standing there in complete terror,
shaking from head to toe, your hands wringing with sweat, your
mouth dry as cotton and right in that moment, you found yourself
in the hub of the biggest faith building experience of your life. You
are in complete and utter amazement while being an eyewitness as
God opens the mouth of the Sea while you stroll across to the other
side of fear. All you had to do was trust God and obey, to make a
decision to take Him at His Word.

Fear in God brings about faith because you believe God will
do what He says He is going to do. God told Moses to raise his
staff and the sea would part. Moses raised his staff as the sea
gathered its waves, stretched out its arms and bared the floor of
its adobe. Remember, Hebrews 11:7 (NIV) says, "By faith Noah,
when warned about things not yet seen, in holy fear built an ark to

save his family. By his faith he condemned the world and became heir of the righteousness that comes by faith." The fear of the Lord actually saved mankind; the whole human race was saved because Noah took God at His Word.

After I re-read this passage, a question came to my mind, so I decided to ask God. The question was, "How did Noah condemn the world and become an heir to righteousness?" For some of you, this may be irrelevant, and for others, it may be common knowledge, but for me the answer I received was nothing short of spectacular. Noah condemned the world through the hundred twenty years it took to build the ark. Genesis 6:11-18 (NIV), "Now the earth was corrupt in God's sight and was full of violence. God saw how corrupt the earth had become, for all the people on earth had corrupted their ways. So God said to Noah, 'I am going to put an end to all people, for the earth is filled with violence because of them. I am surely going to destroy both them and the earth. So make yourself an ark of cypress wood; make rooms in it and coat it with pitch inside and out. This is how you are to build it: The ark is to be 450 feet long, 75 feet wide and 45 feet high. Make a roof for it and finish the ark to within 18 inches of the top. Put a door in the side of the ark and make lower, middle, and upper decks. I am going to bring floodwaters on the earth to destroy all life under the heavens, every creature that has the breath of life in it. Everything on earth will perish. But I will establish my covenant with you, and you will enter the ark - you and your sons and your wife and your sons' wives with you.'"

The ark was 450 feet long, 75 feet wide and 45 feet high. It was built on dry ground, not only dry ground but a ground that had never seen rain. Every day Noah and his family worked on building the ark for the upcoming flood. Every day as they gathered their cypress wood, made their pitch, and began their journey of faith, I could only imagine how they were mocked. With each strike of the nail, Noah was condemning the world, declaring guilt. With each coat of pitch, Noah was condemning the mockers, the naysayers and the unbelievers. With each piece of wood which was strategically placed as part of the ark, Noah was condemning the world. With each animal that entered the ark two by two, Noah was condemning the world and becoming an heir to righteousness according to God.

How can we afford not to fear God? How can we go about our lives and live as though fearing everything from being in a car wreck down to getting cancer is acceptable, but fearing God is absurd? Readers, we must take God at His Word; if He says it, then so be it. We have left too much room for the interpretation of fear. Should we not tremble at His Word? Isaiah 66:1-2, 'Heaven is my throne, and the earth is my footstool. Where is the house you will build for me? Where will my resting place be? Has not my hand made all these things, and so they came into being?' declares the Lord. 'This is the one I esteem: he who is humble and contrite in spirit, and trembles at my word.'" Wow! The ones who God esteems are humble, not proud or arrogant, and contrite in spirit. They are regretful and show sorrow for their sins and tremble at His Word. What is your reaction when you read God's Word? Do you read it with the undertones of a man who wrote the Bible or God Himself who wrote the Bible? I believe this question is relevant, because I believe many of us do not tremble at God's Word because we tend to forget that every word in the Bible was inspired by God. God spoke it and man recorded it. There is a hidden danger in operating your life under a false pretense that man wrote the Bible without the knowledge that God inspired every word that was written.

What if we witnessed the same sea opening experience Moses did which allowed him to pass through and then swallowed his enemies whole, digesting the idea of defeat without a moment of remorse? Many of us have chosen the desire to go back to Egypt because the walk of obedience has become a faith issue much more than the physical ability to put one foot in front of the other. We allow ourselves to be bound by our emotions and by our past. Many of you are more comfortable living in Egypt than packing your bags for the promise land. You have become quite comfortable in your misery and it has become your security blanket, your comfort food of sorts, and your identity.

Have you ever heard anyone say, "I am a victim of abuse"? I have on many occasions; that's because being a victim is who they have become. They have dedicated a chair in their home where they sit and cover themselves with the blanket called martyr, they prop their feet upon the stool of defeat and they read from a book called my past, subtitled - pain, hurts, and injustices. You will find them there often, wrapped up and cuddled in the sins of someone else while they dwindle away in a shell of who they once were before the abuse. They have set up camp on the cares of yesterday and meditate on how people have treated them. Readers, welcome to Egypt. If you refuse to move forward today, then your today becomes your tomorrow. Too many tomorrows steal what you have today.

I hear people say things like I have ADD, HDD, ADHD, or HDTV. ☺ I have also heard people say ridiculous things like, "My anxiety keeps me from going here or there." Excuse me, *"your anxiety"* doesn't keep you from going here or there. It's your refusal to get the heck out of Egypt that keeps you from enjoying your life. We have the same power Jesus had to raise people from the dead; why aren't we taking back our authority? Another conversation I have been hearing from blood bought Christians is about *"their depression."* Why do we insist on nailing our tent pegs on the opposite end of what the Word of God says? Come on readers, read your Bible! Get a fresh revelation on the written Word of God! Refuse to live in the dung of Egypt any longer, pack up your bag, dig up your rusted tent pegs, scoop up your flour mill and yeast, grab your clay pots and head out to the promise land! Quit saturating yourself with rancid oil and find out who you are in Christ. Remember what I have said before, if you don't find out who you are in Christ, you will become someone you were never meant to become. ***All of this because we refuse to move forward yesterday.***

So many people are addicted to an identity. It could be an identity such as what we discussed above, anxiety, or depression, or it could be an identity like doctor, lawyer, nurse, minister, preacher, or teacher. The greatest identity I have is that I am a daughter of the Most High. This is where I find my true identity; anything else is fading, fleeting, and a false sense of security. Noah knew who he was in Christ and he knew if God called him to build an ark on dry ground, on a ground that had never experienced rain before then, that same God would supply every need to correlate with His demands and would also bring rain and righteousness.

Another wonderful story about crossing over is found in Joshua 2:1-2, "Then Joshua son of Nun secretly sent two spies from Shittim. 'Go, look over the land,' he said, 'especially Jericho.' So they went and entered the house of a prostitute named Rahab and stayed there."

Readers, as I read through the Scripture I thought to myself, Wow! I noticed the word "then." *Then* Joshua sent two spies over. The word "*then*" led me to ask what happened before. *Then* Moses took his last breath. God told Joshua, "Now *then,* you and all these people get ready to cross the Jordan into the land I am about to give you." God went on to tell them every place they placed their foot was theirs, no one would be able to stand against them; as He was with Moses, He was with them. God furthermore said, "I will never leave you or forsake you. Be strong and courageous, because you will lead these people to inherit the land I swore to the generations before them." In addition, God told them not to let the law depart from their mouth; meditate on it day and night, so they would be careful to do everything that is written. *Then* you will be prosperous and successful. "Do not be afraid for I the Lord God I am with you wherever you go. [28]" So Joshua went through the camp commanding the people to get their supplies ready—"three days from now, we are going to take the land." Joshua 1:16, "*Then* they answered Joshua, 'Whatever you have commanded us we will do, and wherever you send us we will go.'"

To be transparent, readers, I don't understand why Joshua waited three days to cross over when God clearly said get ready and go. God went into great detail how He was going to be with them, but yet they still waited three days until they could receive their, *THEN* moment. Has God spoken a "*then*" moment into your life, but you still find yourself standing on the wrong side of the Jordan? What is holding you back? I noticed the spies were sent to a prostitute's house where they stayed. Listen readers, you don't want to miss the lesson flowing in between the pages of God's miraculous Word. The first lesson was the spies had to believe what God had said to them to actually go to the walls of Jericho, and secondly, the prostitute, Rahab, had to not let her past mistakes keep her from future blessings. Rahab had to refuse to let **yesterday's mistakes keep her from moving forward today.** God had a new script for her with new lines for her to recite. She helped the spies, and in turn, she was written into the hall of faith book in Hebrews 11:31. In one act of faith, she became a part of the genealogy of Jesus written in Matthew 1:5.

After reading this chapter, I quickly figured out that fear and lack of faith keep most people on the wrong side of the Jordan. In order to get to the promise land, we *have* to cross over the Jordan. Readers, don't allow your *THEN* moment to become a *never* moment by the choices you make. I remember a moment when we were in the military, right before we received our first orders to California, God spoke a *then* time in my life. God said many things, but after those things were said, He said, "Then when you get to California there will be a mother figure waiting for you. She will comfort you and become your friend while you are stationed there without your mother." Listen readers, when we arrived there, my spiritual antenna was on high alert. I think it was about the third or fourth day we were in our apartment, as I was walking down the sidewalk, I met my neighbor. Her name was Joni. I told her the Word I had received and it witnessed to her spirit. She and my mom had two things in common, their names and me. God was absolutely right. She was all He said she would be and more. I could have missed my *then* moment had I not believed God and been aware of His Word coming to pass. I was expecting her.

Are you expecting God to do what He says He will do? "Then" moments only come when you won't settle for anything less than what God has for you, when you decide **not to refuse to move forward from yesterday.**

> *Acts 3:1-8 says, "One day Peter and John were going up to the temple at the time of prayer - at three in the afternoon. Now a man crippled from birth was being carried to the temple gate called Beautiful, where he was put every day to beg from those going into the temple courts. When he saw Peter and John about to enter, he asked them for money. Peter looked straight at him, as did John. Then Peter said, 'Look at us!' So the man gave them his attention, expecting to get something from them. Then Peter said, 'Silver or gold I do not have, but what I have I give you. In the name of Jesus Christ of Nazareth, walk.' Taking him by the right hand, he helped him up, and instantly the man's feet and ankles became strong. He jumped to his feet and began to walk. Then he went with them into the temple courts, walking and jumping, and praising God."*

A couple of things went through my mind as I read this passage, such as, why didn't anyone ever take this man inside the Beautiful

Gate, into the temple where there was prayer and worship going on? They placed him outside the Gate called Beautiful, given it was the busiest entrance where he would make the most money, but really his needs far outweighed silver and gold. The passage says the crippled man was put outside the Gate every day. EVERY DAY to receive just enough to get by on. The Word never says he had enough from yesterday to skip a day. No! He was taken there every day to receive just enough to survive another day.

I see this all the time sitting in the church pews, people who come every Sunday just to get enough of God's Word to make it until next Sunday, *just enough* to get by on. They don't open their Bibles during the week. They don't pray to their God during the other six days. They are living on *just enough* to get by and they have resorted to a *just enough* mentality. I talk to people every day who are living in their past, accepting *just enough* healing to get through another day, not enough to be whole, well, or restored but *just enough* to get by on. **Refusing to move forward yesterday** will keep you living in your past, whatever that past is. It could be your past sin, the past sins of someone else or past regrets.

How many of you are settling for *just enough* in your marriages? You say things like, "Well, my marriage isn't perfect but no one else's is either." Just drop another coin in the bucket, go ahead, sit outside the beautiful gate and settle for *just enough* love to get by on, not enough to thrive, not enough to shine, *just enough* to stay together. How many of my readers have settled on superficial relationships with their parents? You are still wounded from your childhood, walking around with *just enough* forgiveness to stand to be around them for the Holidays. Many of you are taking care of your kids *just enough* not to have them taken away; you're feeding them, clothing them, sending them to school, but because you're broken, you're not loving them the way they need to be loved. You are **refusing to move forward yesterday**.

Some of you reading this book are doing drugs *just enough* to get by on, not enough to overdose on, but *just enough* to be checked out. I was raised by a mother who had a heroin addiction. It was extremely painful to know you have a mother, who many times, picked drugs over you. Listen, why are you settling for *just enough* when Jesus came to give you **more than enough**? How many times are you going to let the silver and gold drop in the bucket before you enter into the beautiful gate? How long are you going to let your life represent the lame? Many of you are lying outside the gate of God's provision, stretching your buckets out in hopes of one piece of silver to cling to the bottom.

We serve a God who is more than enough, yet many of us live as if *just enough* will suffice. It's selfishness. Do you know what you would have to offer others if you would walk in more than enough love, forgiveness, joy, healing, restoration, reconciliation, hope, patience and kindness? Do not set up your tent outside the gate called Beautiful. Go in, walk the walk of faith, believing your God will meet you at the altar. Be healed, restored and renewed by His presence. **Don't refuse to move forward from yesterday's events and remain the same.**

Choices are for the Living:

1. How do you respond to God's Word?

   _____
   _____
   _____
   _____
   _____
   _____
   _____
   _____
   _____
   _____
   _____
   _____
   _____

2. What kind of hypothetical Ark has God ask you to build? Have you started?

   _____
   _____
   _____
   _____
   _____
   _____
   _____
   _____
   _____
   _____
   _____
   _____
   _____

3. Who do you believe wrote the Bible?

_____
_____
_____
_____
_____
_____
_____
_____
_____

4. Are you expecting God to do anything right now in your life? Why or Why not?

_____
_____
_____
_____
_____
_____
_____
_____
_____

5. Is there a situation in your life right now that you're refusing to move forward in? What steps can you take to start moving in a positive direction?

_____
_____
_____
_____
_____
_____

Michele Davenport

Weekly Challenge: Write down three things you can do to move forward from yesterday.

1.

_____

_____

_____

_____

_____

_____

2.

_____

_____

_____

_____

_____

_____

3.

_____

_____

_____

_____

_____

_____

Additional Notes:

_____
_____
_____
_____
_____
_____
_____
_____
_____
_____
_____
_____
_____

Michele Davenport

Chapter 12

Now Choose Life

Deuteronomy 30:19, "This day I call heaven and earth as a witnesses against you that I have set before you life and death, blessings and curses. **Now choose life,** *so that you and your children may live."*

C hoices are for the living and your choice will invite God into your decision. I believe God has set life and death, blessing and curses before us to choose. The life we choose will bring about blessings or curses upon us and our children. I know God offers grace, and I believe in the grace of God, but I also believe there are consequences for our decisions. I will lose many of you in my final chapter due to this thing called grace. There will be a few who will hang with me, but for the most part, many will let their eyes slide off the page into a land where Grace is your escape clause. You know who you are, the ones that say things like it really doesn't matter what I choose, if I miss God, He will redirect me. His grace has me covered. Although you are right in some aspects of your thinking, it has become your handicap by your willingness to quit seeking the answers only He can give, because you know His grace abounds. The same thing that brings you peace can allow you to become complacent.

It all started in the garden with one choice. Genesis 2:16-17, "And the Lord God commanded the man, 'You are free to eat from any tree in the garden; but you must not eat from the tree of the knowledge of good and evil, for when you eat of it you will surely die." I just now caught something I had never seen before in this passage, and although I know God is all knowing, I just realized the word God chose to use was "When" you eat of it you will surely die." God said "when." He knew Adam and Eve were going to make the wrong choice, but He still allowed them to choose and God will still allow you to choose the wrong decisions...but there will be consequences. What decisions will you make when given the choice? Essentially, Adam and Eve chose death. Let me ask you a question, did God have grace on Adam and Eve after they ate from the forbidden tree? Yes, God did, but sin was still introduced into the world and through their sin, man was condemned and a Savior had to die.

Cain had a choice to make when sin came crouching at his door. Genesis 4:3-7, "In the course of time Cain brought some of the fruits of the soil as an offering to the Lord. But Abel brought fat portions from some of the firstborn of his flock. The Lord looked with favor on Abel and his offering, but on Cain and his offering he did not look with favor. So Cain was very angry, and his face was downcast. Then the Lord said to Cain, 'Why are you angry? Why is your face downcast? If you do what is right, will you not be accepted? But if you do not do what is right, sin is crouching at your door; it desires to have you, but you must master it.'"

Most of us know the story. Sin did come crouching at Cain's door and Cain did not do what was right; he killed his brother. Many of you reading this, including myself, have had sin crouching at our door before. Sometimes we chose the right answer, and other times, we have chosen the wrong answer. God's grace did abound, but there were still consequences for our choices. I read somewhere that we get to choose the sin but not the consequence. Just knowing there will be a consequence should cause us to saturate our decision with a little more prayer and less rationalizing. If you read on in Genesis, God gave Cain his consequence. He told him that he was going to be a restless wanderer on the earth. I have seen many people who fit this description. They wander around just living life, not really making a difference for the kingdom of God. The choices they make are worldly; they make decisions that only apply in the now. Choices are for the living – do what is right.

Abraham had to choose to listen to God when He told him he was going to be the father of many nations. In Genesis 12:1-2, "The Lord had said to Abram, 'Leave your country, your people and your father's household and go to a land I will show you. I will make you into a great nation and I will bless you; I will make your name great, and you will be a blessing." Choices are for the living, and if God has made you a promise that you would be a mother or father, choose to believe.

Nehemiah made a choice to mourn the fallen walls of Jerusalem which led him into action. "The wall of Jerusalem is broken down, and its gates have been burned with fire. When I heard these things, I sat down and wept. For some days I mourned and fasted and prayed before the God of heaven" (Nehemiah 1:3-4).[29] "So the wall was completed on the twenty-fifth of Elul, in fifty-two days" (Nehemiah 6:15).[30] Choices are for the living - rebuild the heart that has been broken.

Naaman had to make a choice to go dip his body in the dirtiest river to receive his healing. He dipped one, two, three, four, five, six, and on the seventh time, he came out a mud pie, but he was cleansed of leprosy. "Elisha sent a messenger to say to him, 'Go wash yourself seven times in the Jordan, and your flesh will be restored and you will be cleansed' (2 Kings 5:10)."[31] Choices are for the living - do what the Lord tells you to do and be cleansed.

The ten virgins each had a choice to make. Five chose to be ready by bringing their lamps and their oil for the wedding. Five chose to bring lamps with no oil. The oil represents our own spiritual condition; five were well prepared for the groom coming for his bride and five were empty spiritually. "At that time the kingdom of heaven will be like ten virgins who took their lamps and went out to meet the bridegroom. Five of them were foolish and five were wise. The foolish ones took their lamps but did not take any oil with them. The wise, however, took oil in jars along with their lamps" (Matthew 25:1-4).[32] Choices are for the living - choose to fill up with the Word of God.

There was a famine in the land and Elijah could have starved to death had he chosen not to listen to the voice of the Lord. "Go at once to Zarephath of Sidon and stay there. I have commanded a widow in that place to supply you with food" (1 Kings 17:9).[33] The widow and her son could have died a horrible death of starvation and dehydration in the desert if she would have made the wrong choice. 1 Kings 17:14, "For this is what the Lord, the God of Israel, says: 'The jar of flour will not be used up and the jug of oil did not run dry until the day the Lord gives rain on the land.'" Choices are for the living - choose to "go."

Peter and John had a choice to make. They stopped at the Gate of Beautiful and offered Jesus to the lame, when everyone else only offered alms to the lame at the gate. Acts 3:6, "Then Peter said, 'Silver and gold I do not have, but what I have I give you. In the name of Jesus Christ of Nazareth walk.' Taking him by the right hand, he helped him up, and instantly the man's feet and ankles became strong." Choices are for the living - offer someone Jesus.

Mary, the mother of Jesus, had to choose to allow the angel Gabriel to speak life into her body, to proclaim the answer to sin in the world. Mary's response was, "May it be to me as you have said" (Luke 1:38). Choices are for the living - go ahead, give birth to what God has called you to carry.

Rahab chose to hang a red cord out of her window so her whole household would be saved.[34] Choices are for the living - go ahead do something radical for the saving of your household.

The priest made a choice to stick a foot in the Jordan and the water stood on its head (Joshua 3:13). Choices are for the living - stick a toe in whatever God has called you to walk through.

Joshua walked his armed men around Jericho for six days in silence and on the seventh day they marched around the city seven times while the priests were blowing their trumpets. Then the people gave a loud shout as the wall around the city collapsed, just as the Lord told Joshua it would.[35] Choices are for the living - choose to go where God calls you to go, and stay as long as He has called you to stay.

Readers, are we making a difference with the choices we make?

I have by no means exhausted all the people in the Bible who made the choice to choose the right thing. As I have already mentioned in Chapter Eleven, Noah had a choice when God said build an ark. He could have looked at God and said, "What? You want me to build an ark to prepare for a flood when it's never even rained before?" But the Word of God spoke to Noah.[36] Then in Genesis 6:22, the Word of God says Noah did everything just as God told him to.

Noah was a great storm survivor. After God shut the doors to the ark, He told Noah to stay in there for seven days. On the seventh day, the Lord brought the rain for forty days and nights. As one inch turned into two, everything seemed to be the same, except Noah and his family were locked inside an ark with 2 of every kind of animal. As the animals tried to settle into their new surroundings, Noah became innately sensitive of the waters rising. With each passing minute, it seemed life as he knew it was drawing to an end.

I can imagine day one was filled with curiosity of the rain, since it had never rained before. I'm confident people were intrigued with its slippery wet feel, how it smelled, how it seemed to wash the day's debris off with ease. I know some were thinking ahead and collecting the wet substance coming from above to use at a later time. I'm certain the world's atmosphere was changing, not only in the physical but in the spiritual as well. As day two arrived and the rain was still coming down, there were probably a few who thought back on the words of Noah and wondered secretly if there could be any truth to the ark and its purpose. As the noise of the children splashing around filled Noah's ears, his heart was certainly breaking for mankind. Day three only brought about a sense of urgency for it to be over, but yet the trauma of the storm was just beginning. As the days turned into weeks, the horror of reality was finally sinking in. The screams were piercing the ears of the living, the wailing of parents watching their children being swept away by the raging storm. The husbands desperately trying to keep their wives above the flood waters only to watch them drown before their very eyes. The wives watching their men as the water opened its mouth and swallowed them whole. The devastation could not be escaped, the water was playing hide and seek but there was nowhere to hide that the water could not find you. As it tortured you, played with you as if to let you catch your breath long enough to give you hope, but then held you hostage, feeding you only what fish could endure without death.

I can't help but wonder what they may have been thinking in those moments right before the water became their grave. Was Noah right, was his God right? When you're reading the story of Noah, it's almost like you can hear the cries of doubt and unbelief bubbling up from the ground. Finally, after 40 days and nights, what must have seemed like eternity to Noah and his family as they stood inside the grace of God, the earth became silent. The rain stopped and started to recede. The world, at last, starts to drink up the waters as if it was in the middle of the Sahara Desert without a canteen. With one belch, Noah's ark landed on top of a mountain. It is here where I found the greatest miracle. Noah and his family became survivors of the largest storm this world has ever witnessed. What is the first thing you do after a bad storm? You step out and do inventory of the damage. You look around and write down everything that is broken. Noah could have stepped out of the ark and started taking inventory of all that was lost. He could have said, "Wow! Everything is gone. There is no one left but us, all the animals not on the ark have disappeared. Every living thing that had breath has vanished. We're all alone. What are we going to do with this enormous earth?" Noah could have taken inventory of what was lost, but here is the miracle--he chooses to take an inventory of what God had saved. God had saved him and his whole family.

In light of how Noah chose to look at this situation, it's not surprising what Noah did as soon as he stepped out of the ark.

He built an altar of praise. Noah's praise was at such a place that God responded to him with these words. Genesis 8:21b, "Never again will I curse the ground because of man." Our praise is our testimony. When you can praise from this place, God will say, never again. Never again will you go through depression, never again will you pick up drugs, never again will you light another cigarette, never again will you struggle with self infliction and never again will you fall into lust, because who I have set free is free indeed.[37] When Noah made a choice to build an altar of praise, God said "Never again." We can choose to live in Egypt or we can choose to praise God.

Choices are for the living - live to praise.

To end this book without giving you the opportunity to make the greatest choice you can ever make would be insane. If you haven't received the Lord as your personal Savior, make a choice to pray this prayer. Choices are for the living, but if you don't choose while you're alive, the choice will be made for you after you die. God will not resurrect you out of hell.

> Roman 10:9 says, "That if you confess with your mouth, 'Jesus is Lord,' and believe in your heart that God raised him from the dead, you will be saved."

Lord, I am confessing with my mouth that You are Lord, and I believe with all my heart that You raised Jesus from the dead. I now ask You to come live in me, forgive me, and paint the canvas of my life as white as snow. Wash away my sins and deliver me from the heartache of my past. Let me extend the same forgiveness as You have extended to me. Lord, also guide my brush that I would only use the color palette of white, as I too, will paint on the canvases of others, affecting what they become. Amen.

Write the date and time of your confession as your faith builder for the future.

Date: _____ Time: _____

Choices are for the Living ...what is your choice?

Choices are for the Living

1. Have you had a garden experience with God? Was there grace in your outcome?

   _____
   _____
   _____
   _____
   _____
   _____
   _____
   _____
   _____
   _____
   _____
   _____

2. What sin is crouching at your door?

   _____
   _____
   _____
   _____
   _____
   _____
   _____
   _____
   _____
   _____
   _____
   _____

3. What is your plan not to fall for the temptation in your life?

_____
_____
_____
_____
_____
_____
_____
_____
_____
_____
_____
_____
_____

4. What promises has God made you?

_____
_____
_____
_____
_____
_____
_____
_____
_____
_____
_____
_____

Michele Davenport

5. What has God asked you to do? What was your response? Was your response, "May it be as you have said"?

_____
_____
_____
_____
_____
_____
_____
_____
_____
_____
_____
_____
_____
_____

Weekly challenge: Lead someone to the Lord; walk them through the sinner's prayer.

Romans 10:9 (TNIV), "If you declare with your mouth, 'Jesus is Lord,' and believe in your heart that God raised him from the dead, you will be saved. For it is with your heart that you believe and are justified, and it is with your mouth that you profess your faith and are saved."

Additional Notes:

_____
_____
_____
_____
_____
_____
_____
_____
_____
_____
_____
_____
_____
_____
_____
_____
_____
_____
_____
_____
_____
_____
_____
_____
_____
_____
_____
_____
_____
_____
_____
_____

Painted Colors

All through my life I have been painted different colors

Some for me, some for others

In the far distance I heard you calling my name

Within the season I would be changed

All alone I open my heart

That's all you needed to make a start

You came right in and made a home

Where you cleansed me, healed me, and called me your own

You stayed with me while I cried my tears

And comforted me through my fears

Fears that I was forever lost,

Fears I would pay the final cost

Death by fire was where I was at,

But I looked different from where you sat

You could see a child, who needed you,

You could see a child broken in two

Through the seasons you chipped away all the old paint

And colored me the color as one of your saints

The color of righteousness, which is white as snow,

Now you're with me wherever I go

Thank you Lord for chipping away the old paint,

Then with Your mercy, You marked me one of Your saints

Michele Davenport

I confess that some of my life colors were not attractive. Some were due to the fault of others, as they dipped their brushes from the color palette of this world, and some were due to me, because I chose to dip my own brush and paint myself in the lies I chose to believe. Before long, I was no longer on the canvas of my own life. I was on the canvas of other people's thoughts and opinions as well as my own distorted view. My color had changed. I let the food of this world almost starve me to death, leaving me in an anorexic state. I allowed for more than one artist to create my self-portrait.

As I made the choice to dedicate my life to God, I grew in wisdom, faith and fear of the Lord. I started noticing my canvas looking different. The old colors were fading away. In my mind, I was standing in an art gallery. There were hundreds of thousands of paintings, but in the distance, there was a silhouette of a Man holding a paintbrush. As I watched in silence, I noticed the painting He was working on was me. He was dipping His brush into a satin white finish, the purest, whitest white I had ever seen. He was repainting, recreating, and reconstructing what the world had painted. With one stroke of His brush, I was washed new and in right standing with my God. In a moment, I was made whole.

Choices are for the Living ...what is your choice?

Michele Davenport

Appendix

(Endnotes)

Chapter 1

USA Weekend, August22-24, 1997, "Fear: What Americans Are Afraid of Today"

Matthew 25:40 NIV

3

Chapter 2

Revelation 2:7 The Message

ESV, Revelation footnotes, commentator Dennis E. Johnson, PhD, Westminster Seminary California

Revelation 2:3 NIV

Revelation 2:10 NIV

The Preacher's Homiletic Commentary Volume 30 page 460

Revelation 2:24 NIV

Revelation 2:25 NIV

1 Timothy 1:6 NKJV

Revelation 3:8 NKJV

12

Chapter 3

Forbes - www.forbes.com

Matthew 22:37 NKJV

Isaiah 6:1 – 4 NIV

Luke 16:24 NIV

According to www.globalissues.org/article/26/poverty-facts-and-stats#src1

Chapter 4

Matthew 1:38 NIV

19

Chapter 5

1 Kings 17:15 – 16 NIV

1 Kings 17:17 – 24 NIV

Chapter 7

KJV Hebrew-Greek Key Word Study Bible Strong's number 4412

[2] Reference taken from "Sparkling Gems from the Greek," by Rick Renner page778

22

If you are interested in volunteering in Allison's ministry "Beautician on a Mission," you can reach her at www.beauticianonamission.com

Chapter 8

www.allaboutfollowingjesus.org - **Voice of the Martyrs**

Romans, 1 and 2 Corinthians, Galatians, Ephesians and Colossians Chapters 1:1

Chapter 10

John 2:19-21(NIV)

Scripture references-Psalm 34:18, Proverbs 3:24, Isaiah 9:6, Jeremiah 31:3, John 8:36, Romans 8:1- 2,

2 Corinthians 1:3-7 and 5:17, Philippians 4:7, Colossians 3:13

Chapter 11

Joshua 1:1-9 NIV

Chapter 12

Nehemiah 1:3b – 4 NIV

Nehemiah 6:15 NIV

2 Kings 5:10 NIV

Matthew 25: 1 – 13 NIV

1 Kings 17:9 NIV

Joshua 2:17-20 The Message

Joshua 6:3-5 NIV

Genesis 6:13-14 NIV

John 8:36 NIV

Please enjoy a few chapters from the other two books Michele has written.

The first one, "*Ripened on the Vine,*" is a true story of Michele's life as she endured emotional, physical, mental and sexual abuse of her past. Walk with her as she learns how to find vertical faith in a horizontal world. The book is really not about her, but more about the One who created her and saved her from death so many times.

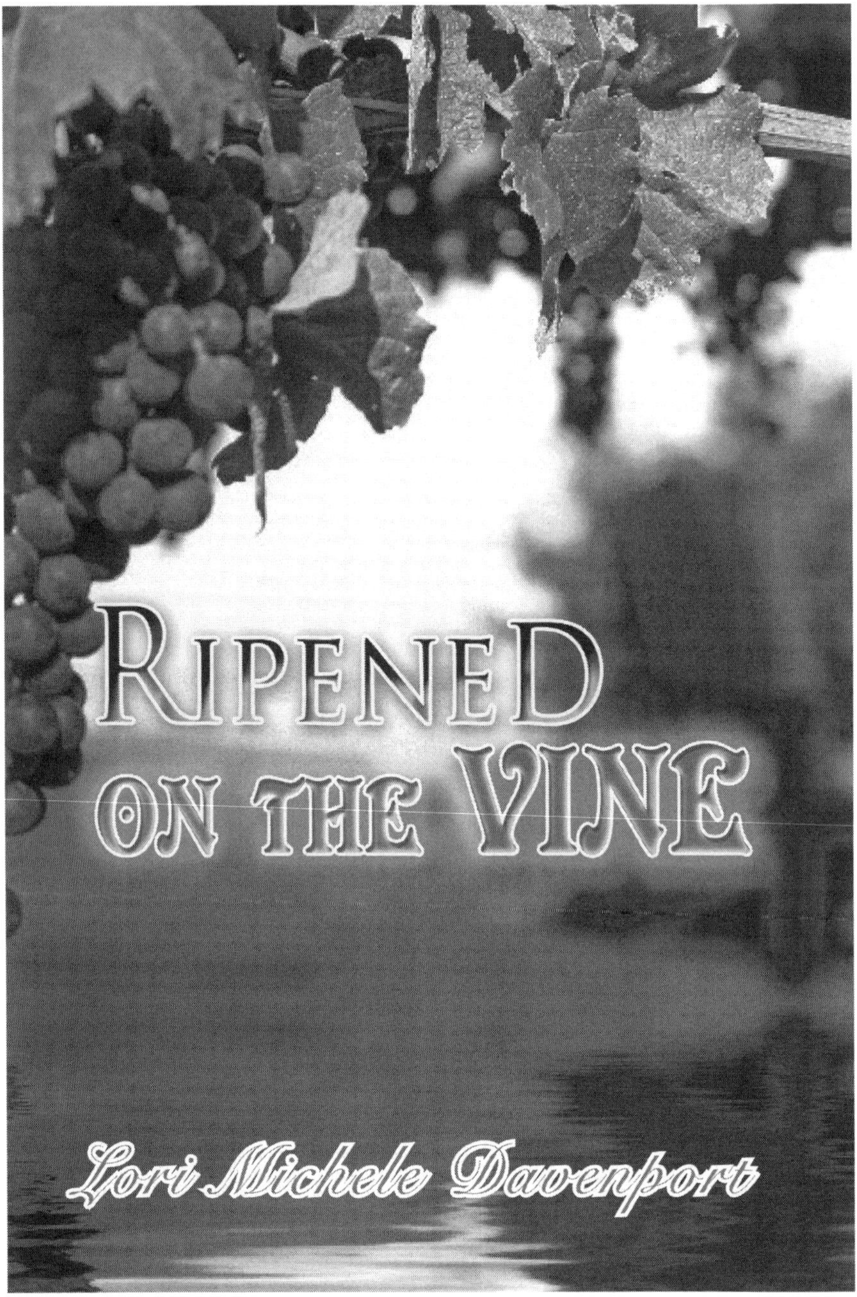
RIPENED
ON THE VINE
Lori Michele Davenport

Chapter One

The Seed In Me

I'm like a flower, and You planted the seed...

You were watching me grow into becoming me...

Making mistakes along the way...

Struggling to hear what my Father has to say...

Closing my eyes and searching my heart...

Finding the place where I needed to start...

At the beginning is a good place to be,

but in the middle is where you will find me...

I'm like a flower and You planted the seed...

Hello, my name is Michele. I dedicate my story to anyone who has ever had a reason to give up on life and God. My heart's desire is for people to be encouraged, not by my life, but by what God has done through my life. This book is not about me. It is about the One who created me, and saved me from death so many times. I once heard a preacher, Myles Munroe, say, "God salvages (saves) people and puts them back together so He can use them for what He originally planned on using them for."

What I was born to do caused God to save me. God has a plan for all of us, and He will save you, too. God has revealed to me that my childhood and my life have been faith builders. He has used them to strengthen my faith in Him.

Lord God, please guide my hands and heart as I begin to tell my life story to all who need a little faith. Thank you, Lord, for never leaving me alone, for being faithful in salvaging me to glorify You.

I was in bed sleeping when I was awakened by a loud noise. I wasn't sure what it was. I saw my dad's face. He got me out of bed. My brother wasn't there that night. He was at my uncle's house where my dad was staying because my parents were separated. He took me into the living room where I saw the front door lying in the middle of the room. He had kicked it completely down. He sat me in the corner, and made me watch as he started to beat my mom. He had been drinking and the odor of beer and cigarettes surrounded him. I was only 4 years old. That was the earliest memory of my dad. It was the only one that I would have for a long time. After he got finished beating her almost to death, he raped her in front of me. I cannot possibly tell you the impression, the visions, the distorted idea of love that was embedded in my mind that night. I was so young and all I could think was that my dad was killing my mom. The last two years of their marriage, my dad began to drink a lot and go out to the bars. He also did some drugs.

Throughout their whole marriage, he beat her and fooled around. After he had left that evening, my mom found the strength to call my grandmother. She came and picked us up and took us to the hospital. My mom was so badly beaten that the doctors did not know, and could not tell my grandmother, if my mom would live or die. The state attorney's representative came by to take my mom's statement, but she was in a coma. Her neck looked like she had been strangled, and since she was in a coma, they could not get all the facts. Later, they found out that my dad did this with his bare hands. The marks on her neck were unbelievable. It looked like someone had put a rope around her and tried to choke her. The officers could not believe the damage my dad had done.

I do not remember how long my mom was in the hospital. After my mom got out, we went to live with my grandma. We had to pass that apartment every day and I would say, "That is where it happened, Mom, isn't it?" The memories of what happened were strong in my mind and I did not want to be around my dad.

When my brother found out what had happened to mom, he begged her to drop the charges, and my mom did. Soon after this happened, my dad checked into a mental hospital. Later we found out why my dad decided to have this last revenge on our mother. He found out the divorce would be final in six days, and that was more than he could stand. He went insane that night. After dad got out of the mental hospital, he disappeared in Corpus Christi to hide from paying child support and the police. While in Corpus, he met his future wife. She seemed to keep my dad out of trouble. My parents had married young and divorced young. The first two years of their marriage, Dad got put into prison for burglary. My dad was not a very nice man back then.

Before the divorce, my brother and I used to pray that God would save their marriage. After that night, we prayed that He would never answer that prayer. God had His hands on our lives even before we knew Him. When you pray, and you do not think God has answered your prayers, know that He is God and we might not have the answer we expected, but He gave the answer that was best for us.

As I'm typing this story, I have an amazing chill. Not because of the pain I felt back then, but because of the healing I feel now, and the peace I have with my dad and my mom. The emptiness that followed the years to come was overwhelming at times. I did not realize how important a father figure is in your life until I did not have one, good, bad or indifferent.

Many years later, my mom met a man who was God-sent. His name was Gilbert. It is just amazing how God knows what we need when we need it. This man loved life; he cherished every minute. I'll never forget the family vacations at Garner State Park going camping, horseback riding, rapid riding and dancing. This was truly the family I dreamed about. He was a spur-of-the-moment kind of person, and my mom was a perfectionist. She never wanted to leave anything undone. I can still hear my dad saying, "Joni, you can either stay home and get those dishes done or we can go fishing, but there isn't enough time to do both." The house was always immaculate and he knew it would not hurt her to leave a few dirty dishes. When he said, "It's time to go," that meant he was in the car backing out.

He raced motor-cross at the Astrodome in Houston, Texas. He loved to ride motorcycles. He also liked to be in the crash-up derby contests. This man truly had a love for people and life. He did not have very many rules, but the ones he had, he expected you to obey. He also believed in working hard and being honest. My brother really loved Gilbert. He hadn't had a dad figure in his life for a long time; you could tell the closeness.

Every year, he would take us on vacation to my Aunt Linda's house outside of Corpus Christi at Weber's boat landing. That's where we would go fishing. I remember Richard, my brother, and I getting in the canoe and rowing out to the middle of the lake to go cork fishing, and it started raining and raining. I asked him, "Should we go in?"

He said, "No, this is when the fish really start biting." My brother had the patience of Job when it came to fishing. He did not even have to get a bite all night. He just loved the idea of fishing. That day, I caught more fish than I ever caught in my life, and I have never caught that many fish since.

There was something about my aunt that I loved. She had peace and joy. My aunt did not hesitate to let you know how she felt and what she believed. My aunt is an awesome woman of God and she ministered to my heart. I was blessed with having someone like that to keep the prayer lines open.

Richard and I had so much fun when we were kids. When it flooded, we would make up all kinds of games. One was called *jump the ditch*. Our house sat right beside this ditch. The object was to jump this six-foot ditch without landing in it. I don't think I ever played this game without getting soaked. Also, in the summer months, he would take one side of the road and I would take the other, and we would look inside the meters for toads. We would collect as many as we could find, then return home to see who won.

Richard and I had a good relationship. I would always follow him around, and he would always tell me to stop it. I would tell on him every chance I got, and he did the same to me, but we loved each other. I remember walking down the street in the middle of summer talking to him, asking him all kinds of questions that I thought a big brother ought to know. Sometimes he would answer them, sometimes he would laugh, and sometimes he would tell me to be quiet. When we got into trouble, and that was most of the time, my mom believed in the tattle-tale-and-consequences method of punishment. If you told on someone, you got punished, and the person who did the crime got punished also. It worked out good for her, but we sure were bored. Anyway, when this happened we usually got grounded to our rooms. The rooms were side by side with a big mirror hanging on the wall in between them. We used to make paper airplanes and throw them at each other in the mirror. We also liked to make spit balls and launch them at each other.

Richard liked to play jokes on people. One day, he went on a mission to find as many snakes as he could. When he came back to the house with a shirt full, he walked right in to his room, pulled out his underwear drawer and placed the snakes in there as neatly as he could. Richard went back outside and waited for the moment that he could hear our mom scream.

My mom was doing laundry, and she headed back to Richard's room to put his shirts and socks away. She opened his underwear drawer, and you could have heard her from two states over. She yelled, "Richard Allen, get in this house right now!" That day there was not a tattletale consequence. I don't think he ever did that again. Mom did not think that was funny at all. Years later, it is one of the funniest stories that she tells.

Back then my mom took us to church. She loved the Lord. She wanted to raise her kids with Godly values. I remember my first experience in church. My mom would take us down the street to the local Methodist church. I don't think there was Sunday school, or if there was, my mom did not take us to it. I do know we had to be perfectly still, not a peep or she would pinch us--not just a regular pinch, but a pinch with a twist. To be honest, we got our share of being pinched. As quiet as we had to be, there were a lot of seeds being planted in those years we were in church. I have my mom to thank for that. Although the seeds would not be watered until much later in my life, they were always there. When I think about that, it is amazing to me how powerful our God is. The Scripture says: *He knew me and every hair on my head*. That alone is more than I could ask for, but He gave me so much more--more than I could hope for or dream I could have. Could you imagine the time it would take to know every hair on someone's head? God is faithful.

One night after my brother and I went to bed, we were awakened by a terrible noise. It sounded awful. We got up to see what had happened and my mom was just sitting there crying. For the moment, everything just stood still. We knew it was bad, but we were not prepared for what was about to be unfolded. She began to tell us that our dad had been driving in his dune buggy with a friend. They had been drinking and driving on Galveston Bay wall. It was a steep wall and everyone liked to ride his or her motorcycles, bikes, and dune buggies on it. The wall was about a mile long. They decided to get a bottle and take a ride, but they approached the end sooner than they expected. Dad turned the buggy as sharply as he could. He did not want to go over because there was nothing down there but rocks and ocean. As soon as he turned it, it flipped over, breaking my dad's neck. He died instantly and his friend lived. I don't know why Gilbert had to die that night but I do know, no matter what, God is faithful. God did not cause him die. The lies of Satan did. I can hear Satan saying, "Oh, go ahead and drink and drive, nothing will happen to you. People do it every day." God tells us many times throughout the Bible about obeying.

In Genesis 2:16, "And the Lord God commanded the man, "You are free to eat from any tree in the garden; but you must not eat from the tree of knowledge of good and evil, for when you eat of it you will surely die." Acts 5:29 also says we must obey God rather than men.

We shouldn't depend on man to know what we need. We need to learn to depend on God more and us less. I know if Gilbert would have been conformed into what the Lord wanted for him that night, he would have not been out on that wall driving under the influence. More often than not, we want to be the drivers in our own lives, and then people blame the Lord for what has happened or did not happen. I believe we need to be a people who want to serve the Lord no matter what the cost, but every time we get a little nervous, or out of our comfort zone, we back off.

The Lord said, *keep your eyes focused on my kingdom and Me and everything else will be added unto you.* He came to give us an abundant life, not to kill us. Satan came to kill, steal, and destroy. That is how he works. He makes things look fun that are really dangerous and can kill you. Satan's goal is to kill you before you can find out the truth about the One who came to save you, Jesus. The One who gave His life so you could live.

After that night, everything changed. Where we once had security, we now had none. Our lives were left so empty. I remember when my softball coach came by to sign me up for the season. I just looked at him and said, "My dad died and my mom needs me this year. I won't be playing." I loved softball, but things were not going to be the same, and I knew that even as a small child. I'll never forget how my coach looked at me that day, and he said, "Maybe next year." His eyes were filled with sorrow. I will always remember his sweet spirit.

A year had gone by and our lives would never be the same. Richard was not handling Gilbert's death well at all, and he did not understand why he was taken from us. He had a lot of anger in him towards God and everyone around him. My brother really loved Gilbert. I could see the loss on Richard's face every time I looked at him. It was as if someone had stolen his smile only to replace it with tears of sorrow. It was if my brother lost his only hope of being a part of a real family. The pain that penetrated his entire being was evident in his speech, his walk, his movement; his very soul yearned from a place I had never witnessed before in him. Mom started noticing a change when the school started calling about Richard getting into fights and not turning in his assignments.

It got worse, and he started hanging around the wrong people and doing the wrong things. Drugs became a part of his life, as well as alcohol, and he started smoking. He was getting into a lot more trouble. Our relationship was not the same; he did not want me around, and he started treating me with a lot of hostility.

I know my mother was getting concerned, so when my brother asked if he could go live with my real dad, even though she would have rather he stayed with her, she knew he needed to be around a father figure again so she agreed.

I heard my mom make the phone call that night, and my brother was overjoyed. She knew, better than anyone, my dad had a bad temper and she warned Richard. Richard did not listen. That night he thought mom was just trying to talk hateful about our dad. I knew better, I still remembered that night he broke in. The place I had never witnessed my brother in before was an all too familiar place for me. I knew the pain of loss. I knew the pain of torment. I mourned my own purity of mind due to the things I witnessed as a small child. I could reveal truth to my brother but was he in a place to receive? Would he be able to take another death, not of flesh and blood, but another death of his dreams of ever having a normal family? The answer to these questions and too many more will always remain a mystery because I never could bring myself to plead a case against his hope. I remained silent.

Chapter Two

Wisdom

The sun is shining; it is a new day...

Clouds fill my heart, only words left to say...

God give me the wisdom to understand...

My life is Your life, with only one plan...

I reach up to Heaven calling out Your name...

Oh Lord, be with us through all this change...

Give me the heart to understand...

Give me the wisdom to know Your plan...

It was just my mom and I now, and I could tell she was really lonely and afraid of being without Gilbert. It had been a little over a year and she had started dating. I do not think she was ready, but I don't think she liked being alone. The change in her had come little by little. I started noticing it after she started dating this new man. Although he was sweet on the outside, his insides were torn from the floor up. He had a very cruel side, which we would learn about later. They dated a few months and then decided to get married. The memories of Gilbert filled our house, and he wanted us to start a new life with him so he suggested we move. Plus he had a lot of money and I'm sure he wanted a bigger house. So we moved to another house and began our life with this new man, another step-dad for me. At first our lives seemed good. We had plenty of money and friends. I was popular at school. I played a lot of sports, such as volleyball and basketball, and I was on the track team. All the teachers liked me. Things were good for a while.

I started noticing that there was something strange about my step-dad. He had a weird side to him. My mom did not seem very happy. I think she realized that she got married too fast after Gilbert's death, but she was lonely and thought that my step-dad could fill that void for her. My mother started seeing a psychiatrist every week, but she just wasn't getting any better. I did not understand how this was happening. Later I found out that my step-dad was behind it. He was slowly increasing my mom's medication to get her to do some things she normally would not do. He was sick.

Before long, my mom was in a bad way. She really did not know what was going on most of the time. I do know that he was blackmailing her somehow to stay with him. It did not take long for our house to be known as the party house. To see my mom so out of it on drugs, bothered me. She was who I counted on, and I was losing her to that man and drugs. The loneliness I felt was unbearable. I lived in a house with a mom who did not know I was there and a step-dad who did. He would purposely walk in when I was taking a bath or a shower, and he loved to tickle me in places he shouldn't. I went to school and tried to act like everything was great, but everyone knew better. They had seen my mom and step-dad, and they knew everything was far from being great. Things started to get worse. He had my mom committed.

I think my mom wanted to divorce him. I remember talking to him one time, and I mentioned that I was scared of bugs, especially June bugs. He took a real interest in the things I feared.

One night as I was getting ready for bed, I shut my door, pulled back the covers, and when I did, I saw a lot of June bugs crawling all over my bed. I screamed and cried. I could not believe he did this to me. I could not imagine what entered his mind to make him do such a thing to a child. I wondered what he was thinking when he was collecting all those bugs. Was he thinking how funny it was going to be, or was he thinking how scared I would be, or was he just not thinking. I can tell you this, if you do not have the Lord on your mind and in your heart, Satan can get in. The Bible says, *you are either for me or you are against me.* It is that simple.

I don't know how long my mom was in the mental hospital, but I do remember visiting her. I thought to myself, "Why was my mother there," because she did not act like the other people that I had seen there. I knew that my step-dad was behind all of this, but I could not prove it. My mom came home and everything was back to normal.

One evening, the phone rang and it was a friend I used to hang around with when my dad was alive. She wanted to know if I could go with her and another friend to an amusement park. I asked my mom and she said sure. The next morning my friend's mom came and got me to take us to the park. It took about 30 minutes to get there. She was going to drop us off and pick us up at closing.

We were so excited to be going to this park. When we got there, we paid for our tickets, and I remember making the comment that I wished I had a season pass so I could go anytime I wanted. My friend had one and so did our other friend. We went into the amusement park, and we headed straight for the roller coasters. We rode them for a while and decided to go to the other side of the park. As we were walking, I noticed that a man was following us. I told my friend to watch and see if she thought someone was following us. We would walk into stores, look around, and when we would come out, he would be there. Everywhere we went, he was there. We were only 11 and did not know what to do about it, so we stopped and told the security guard. He said he knew him. He was a police officer. So we decided to go ride some more rides and forget about it. A couple of hours went by, and finally, the man approached us. He wanted to know if we wanted to help catch some bad guys. He showed us his badge, and he assured us that it was okay with our parents; he said he already called them. He also said that if we helped them catch these guys, they would give us one thousand dollars. Rhonda and our other friend thought about it and said no. I was still thinking about it when he also offered a free season pass. I stood there for a few moments and then decided to help. The police officer told Rhonda and our friend to go ride the rides, and we would all meet back there about 5:00 p.m. As I watched them walk away, I was so excited about helping out and getting paid and a season pass that I did not bother to ask what I would be doing.

Moments later, the police officer asked what my address was and phone number.

I was puzzled. I said, "You told me you already talked to my mom and she said it was okay for me to help you." He said, "Oh, I know, I am just confirming so I know where to send the check to," and that sounded okay to me. I was only eleven.

We started walking around almost like we were trying to find someone. Every now and again, he would go and talk to a security guard. He told me they were working with him, and he was checking on information. He seemed really secretive and that scared me. I remember the police officer walking me to a bench and telling me not to move, he had people watching me. He was going to go in the store, and he would be right back. It seem like it took forever, but he came back with a paper bag and a coke. He sat down and offered me a drink. I took a drink of it and it had a funny taste to it. I was starting to have doubts about what was going to happen. I set the coke on the edge of the bench so it would spill. When it did, he got really upset with me. Then he told me to get up and that we needed to walk around so his helpers could get a good look at me, so they would know that I was one of the good guys. He was good. He kept me believing that I was really helping the police. Finally, we approached this place that had been abandoned. The attraction had not been working for months. We went across the bars, and through some trees, down towards a ditch about 6 feet deep.

The police officer told me to sit down on my knees, and he was looking all around from one side to the other. I asked him what he was doing. He said making sure they could see us. I asked, "Who?"

He said, "The people we were helping." Then he opened the bag and pulled out a bandana. I just looked at him. He told me what he was going to do. He said he was going to gag me so we could attract the bad people. At this very moment, I knew this man was going to hurt me. After an hour or so went by, he whispered in my ear, "I am going to leave now. You count to 100 and then you can get dressed and leave." 1-2-3-4-5-6-7-8-9 all the way until I reached one hundred.

As I was kneeling, I realized God had saved me. He was the one untying me. I got up and went looking for this man, but the park was closed. I was determined to find him. Why? For the season pass

- the faith of a child. I still believed, in some sick way, I was helping the police. It would not be until later that I realized what happened to me. The place was really dark, and I was having trouble finding my way to the front gates. It seemed like it took me forever to get where I needed to be. Finally, seeing some light, I heard a woman screaming, "Where is she, what has happened to her, are you going to go look for her?" As I got closer, I realized it was my friend's mom. They were standing there with this awful look on their faces crying and crying. I thought they were upset at me for being late.

After some paperwork and after I told them what happened to me, I think they offered me a season pass. They did not want any unnecessary attention. It would cause panic and certainly was not good for business. I passed on the season pass. It no longer appealed to me. It no longer held the same value as it once did. The place where I went to have fun and be free with my friends, where I escaped some of my pain, now was a part of my pain. I found myself with no place to hide, no place to feel safe, no place to escape the reality of my life.

They took me home and explained to my mom what had happened. I went to take the longest shower I'd ever taken and cried as many tears I could bear to cry. I had never felt as dirty as I did that day. I still did not understand really what happened to me. It went through my mind about a thousand times, what I could have done to change what had happened. My mother made me an appointment with a psychiatrist. When I was introduced to him all I could think was, "Great, another man." *What is he going to do that the others have not already done? What is left of my purity, what is left of my self-worth?* My trust in men by this point was dissipating. I went to the psychiatrist for a while, but I do not think it helped me. He was just a stranger, another stranger in my world of confusion. My mom and I did not talk about it; it hurt my mom too much. Holding it all in sure had its problems later in life for me. Only God knows how I struggled with the pain. I could not stand to be touched by most men for a long time, especially older men. I always thought someone was watching me. I had a lot of fear and based many of my decisions on the fear, the fear of never being able to trust again.

I had nightmares every night. All I could think about was that this man had my address and phone number. He could come get me if they didn't catch him. Weeks went by. I could hardly keep my mind on anything. I was always looking over my shoulder. One day the phone rang and it was the police. They said they had caught him. I was so relieved. Although the memories of him were horrible, at least I didn't have to be scared that he was going to find me and kill me. The police also said that I was really lucky that day at the park because this man did this all over the place. Sometimes he would masquerade as a police officer like he did with me, or sometimes he would masquerade as a superintendent of a school.

The next few months were very hard. I had gone back to school trying to catch up on some of my work. The harder I tried, the worse I felt. I just could not function right. I felt like everyone knew and they were looking at me. I felt as if I should be wearing a sign "Innocence gone." I also felt so stupid for believing that man. Every time I looked in the mirror, I could see him. He was overweight and had a wide nose. He wore his hair parted on the right side. He had fat fingers. I noticed his fingers because I believe I saw a wedding ring, and he was short. I could not take enough showers, and I never did feel clean, no matter what I did. My mind did not seem right. Even when I was awake, I would close my eyes and he would be there, just staring at me. The things he did to me and made me do, literally made me sick to my stomach.

One day when I got home, the phone rang. It was the same officer who called when they caught him. He asked to talk to my mom. All I could hear was her saying, "Okay, how did this happen?" When she got off the phone she was crying she said, "Sit down, Michele, I have something to tell you." Remember when they called and said that they had caught him? Well, he escaped last night." Then she went on to tell me that the officer said this man was highly intelligent. He had escaped many times. He even had jumped from a helicopter once, but he assured my mom he would be caught again. I went hysterical. I could not believe this was happening. I remember asking God *why*? I did not get an answer that night, but I did get one many years later. God is preparing us before the time to do the task. He is not the one who is making us go through the trials, but He is the One who can deliver us from the pain they have caused. He is looking for the unlikely to be the likely.

Matthew's experience points out that each of us, from the beginning, is one of God's works in progress. Much of what God has

Michele Davenport

for us, He gives long before we are able to consciously respond to Him. He trusts us with skills and abilities ahead of schedule. He has made us each capable of being His servant. When we trust Him with what He has given us, we begin a life of real adventure. Matthew could not have known that God would use the very skill he had sharpened as a tax collector to record the greatest story ever lived. God has no less meaningful of a purpose for each of us.

My mom thought it would be good for me to have a friend over to spend the night, so I invited someone. We were just goofing off, having a good time, calling my mom. We had two different phone lines in the house. We would call her and say we want a coke or some chips, and she would laugh. The music was playing loud. We were dancing and my phone rang. I picked it up, and I heard a voice say, "I'm watching you, I know what you're wearing and I'm coming to get you," then the phone went dead. I just stood there. My legs felt like rubber. I could not move.

My friend said, "Who was that on the phone," but before I could answer her, I heard a noise outside my window. It was the bushes, scraping back and forth. I started screaming, and then my friend started screaming. I flew out of my room and there stood my step-dad, laughing and laughing. My mom came running from the other side of the house, and I told her what had happen. She could not believe his sick mind.

A couple of years had passed and I was in my early teens. I was starting to like boys, and I found one who I thought was a nice guy. He went to my school and his parents were pleasant. We started dating, if you can call it that. We went to the movies, together. Our parents would drop us off and pick us up after the movie was over. We held hands to our classroom, and I guess you could say we were going steady. We were just like any other teenagers going steady. We broke up and got back together. We went steady off and on for at least a year. I thought I loved him. He was my first kiss, first boyfriend, and first date.

He was a nice guy, but somehow he got involved with drugs. He didn't just do a little here and there, and he did not start out slow. Within months, he was doing drugs all the time and mostly at my house. His parents would come over looking for him a lot. They would drag him out of our house. He was not getting the drugs there at this time, but eventually he would. I tried to tell him that it was changing him, but his desires to get high all the time overwhelmed him. At times, I think he really wanted to stop, but he did not know how. His mom and dad put him into drug rehab, and he would do well for a while, until he would get out and get around some of his old friends. Our relationship did not last. The drugs were too important and we were way too young to be getting so involved, but I thought I was in love with him.

My step-dad and mom were not getting along, and my mom could not take anymore of him, or his perversion. A few months later, my mom filed for a divorce. Another chapter in my life closed, only to open a more terrifying one.

Michele Davenport

From My Heart to Yours Devotional

Lori Michele Davenport

From My Heart to Yours

I have given you love and forgiveness, through my grace,

All that I ask is you seek My face,

Remember Me when the times get rough,

Be secure in knowing that I am enough,

When my Son rises in the righteous ones, the healing in

Their wings has begun,

You are being strengthened with every passing day,

The bridge between us is our escape,

Built in an arch that covers our sin,

From the flowing waters where you have been,

Cast in the sea without a thought,

My Son has been given; your sins have been bought,

He paid the price, the final cost,

He saved your soul from being lost,

Now I live in you, and you live in Me,

This is My creation, the way I created you to be,

Ephesians 1:7-8,

Michele Davenport

"In Him we have redemption through His blood, the forgiveness of sins, in accordance with the riches of God's grace that He lavished on us with all wisdom and understanding."

Now let's look at the word redemption, *"apotutrosis:* ransom in full, something to loosen (Strong's #629 Gk.)"

God paid the price for us with His Son's blood. God has already loosed us from the hold of the enemy. Why do we keep trying to repay a debt that is paid in full? Would you send a payment on a bill you did not owe? God's grace is sufficient; it is our lack of understanding that keeps us from all that God has to offer.

What debt are you always trying to pay? Why do you feel the need to pay it?

———————————————————————
———————————————————————
———————————————————————
———————————————————————
———————————————————————
———————————————————————
———————————————————————
———————————————————————
———————————————————————
———————————————————————
———————————————————————
———————————————————————
———————————————————————

Rekindle Your Spirit

Are you consumed with all of the tomorrows?
That you are ungrateful for today?

Caught up in this life, forgetting the need to pray.
I wonder when you're alone, do you realize your
Life is not your own.

I am between the silences, in the night, fighting to
Show you the plans I have made for your life,

The things you're saving for will soon fade away.
Lay your treasures up in heaven where they are safe.
The day is short, with limited time.
The seasons are passing with My signs.

Rekindle your spirit then connect it with Mine.
It's not too late I have saved the time.

Psalms 119:36-40,

"Turn my heart towards your statutes and not towards selfish gain. Turn my eyes away from worthless things; preserve my life according to your word. Fulfill your promise to your servant, so that you may be feared. Take away the disgrace I dread, for your laws are good. How I long for your precepts! Preserve my life in your righteousness."

"Precepts" is a very interesting word in Hebrew, *"pigguwd,"* means "mandate, appointed, authorization (Strong's #6490)." God has already authorized to give legal power to us; we just need to receive the power. Our main problem is a receiving problem rather than a giving problem.

When is the last time you asked God for a healing? Did you know the healing was already yours; all you needed to do was receive it? Can you really believe? Can you put your faith in the Word? God sent the Word and turned it into flesh (Jesus).

Captives Free

Watching the sins of my life as they're being
Deleted from Your sight

The wrong I have done, has been washed by your Son
Now I have my chance, I have begun

You had chosen me before I was born
Ripped from this world battered and torn

You spoke to my heart, and made me whole
Then placed Your candle in the midst of my soul.

The fire that burns is my spirit within
To know You more to be Your friend

My memories fade far from the pain
The desires of my heart are not the same.

Remaining still while life passes by
Watching Your people while they live to die

Carelessly counting the souls unseen
Not questioning what they believe

Being content with my safe place
No mercy they find not knowing Your grace.

Oh Lord, give me wisdom a vision to see
When Your Word leaves my mouth, set them free.

Galatians 5:1,
    "Stand fast therefore in the liberty where with Christ hath made
us free, and be not entangled again with the yoke of bondage."

Bondage: *"douleuo*-slavery (Strong's #1397 Gk)." When the enemy tries to constantly remind you of your past mistakes, he is trying to keep you a slave to guilt. If he can keep your focus on your past, then he can keep *his* focus on your future. Repent and go on.

Think about whom you are holding in prison with your own un-forgiveness. Write it down, forgive them, and then be forgiven yourself. Who holds the keys to your prison?

_____
_____
_____
_____
_____
_____
_____
_____
_____
_____
_____
_____

Michele speaks at churches, women's retreats and teaches regularly. To contact the author, you can email her at fbmin02@gmail.com, or to order her other books, go to her web page at fbministries.com.